How the Harvard Business School Changed the Way We View Organizations

How the Harvard Business School Changed the Way We View Organizations

Jay W. Lorsch

BEP

BUSINESS EXPERT PRESS

Leader in applied, concise business books

How the Harvard Business School Changed the Way We View Organizations

Cover design by Charlene Kronstedt

Interior design by Exeter Premedia Services Private Ltd., Chennai, India

First published in 2023 by
Business Expert Press, LLC
222 East 46th Street, New York, NY 10017
www.businessexpertpress.com

ISBN-13: 978-1-63742-530-5 (paperback)
ISBN-13: 978-1-63742-531-2 (e-book)

Business Expert Press Human Resource Management and Organizational Behavior Collection

First edition: 2023

10 9 8 7 6 5 4 3 2 1

This book is dedicated to the early HBS Faculty members who shared the belief that the school's curriculum should include knowledge about the human nature of business organizations: Wallace Brett Donham, the school's second Dean, Lawrence Henderson MD, Elton Mayo, and Fritz J. Roethlisberger. And to Paul R. Lawrence, who led the Organizational Behavior Unit after Roethlisberger.

Description

Listen, observe, test—these three words lie at the heart of a powerful method for businesses' transformation. Behind this method is a deceptively simple idea: managers and management scholars must first take the pulse of a real business, get its case history, diagnose its problems, and only then solve them. Invented by the scholars who launched the Harvard Business School (HBS), this medical model will still cure companies today.

Damningly, during the last 30 years business schools embraced the presumptions of economists, game theorists, and other calculators of abstraction. The solving of real-world, real-time problems has atrophied and stagnated. In this book, *How the Harvard Business School Changed the Way We View Organizations*, renowned scholar and emeritus professor Jay W. Lorsch marshals evidence, history, and insights from his more than 50-year career at HBS to make the case for a return to the medical model—the practices of listening, observing, and testing in which the fields of human relations and organizational behavior are rooted.

By telling the history of the development of his field, Lorsch demonstrates how the medical model emerged in the years before World War II and for decades helped managers, management scholars, and consultants diagnose and solve the problems besetting companies large and small. Explaining the case studies that define the practice, he discusses how the model has been refined and reapplied by later generations and how it can continue to address issues such as diversity, leadership, competition, and optimal corporate board structures.

Keywords

organizational design; history of organizational behavior; diagnosing organizational problems; organizations as systems; contingency theory of organizations; organizational theory; organizational development; human relations

Contents

Testimonials

"In this breakthrough book, renowned Harvard School Business Professor Jay Lorsch makes a powerful case for restoring business research to first-person observation and inductive reasoning rather than relying primarily on statistical analyses that lack real world insight. Working with the world's leadership experts for the past fifty years, Lorsch culminates his remarkable contributions to leadership in this remarkably insightful book. His conclusions will transform business research for decades to come."—**Bill George, Executive Fellow, Harvard Business; Former chair and CEO, Medtronic, and author of** ***True North: Emerging Leader Edition***

"Jay Lorsch is a trailblazer, brilliantly championing the return to the roots of our field by urging deep, insightful diagnoses of organizations. His staunch advocacy for meticulous field research speaks volumes of his ground-breaking influence. A true titan and a dynamic force in organizational behavior, his relentless pursuit of knowledge challenges and inspires us to become informed problem solvers."—**Tsedal Neeley, Naylor Fitzhugh Professor of Business Administration, Harvard Business School**

Acknowledgments

I cannot remember to what Hilary Clinton was referring when she famously said "it takes a village," but she might have been talking about writing a book such as this.

I have had the editorial support of Betsy Seifter, who was married to an MD and grew up in a medical family. Unfortunately, because of health problems in her own family, she had to leave us in 2021. Initially, I also had the support of my research associate, Emily Irving, who was working on a PhD in Organizational Behavior, but after two years of doctoral study at The Harvard Faculty of Arts and Sciences she decided she did not want to get a doctorate and resigned from the university to seek other career opportunities. Her experience at Harvard is similar to that of other doctoral students described in the book.

In spite of these two resignations, I was able to complete the book because of the great help and support I received from Thomas LeBien, a professional editor, whom I was introduced to by one of my colleagues. Thomas has had a profound influence on the book and his editorial work has been invaluable. It was my good fortune that he decided to resign from Harvard University Press and joined Amanda Moon at Moon & Company at the moment I needed his help. Thomas not only provided his own editorial insights and skills but also brought editorial skills from others together to successfully complete the book.

In the field of Organizational Behavior at Harvard Business School, I am also indebted to my colleagues, Tsedal Neeley, Senior Associate Dean of Faculty, for reviewing an early draft of the book, and to Bill George, an early MBA student of mine and later CEO of Medtronics, for reading and commenting on an early draft of the book as well.

I also want to thank my daughter, Robin Lorsch Wildfang, who from her home in Denmark was able to provide the footnotes and help with the writing of the book in other ways. Her education as a PhD, albeit in Classics, gave her particular sympathy for the plight of our graduate students in Organizational Behavior.

I wish to thank my assistant, Elyssa Bjorkman, for the extreme confidence and skill with which she has handled the various administrative and editorial tasks I asked her to do.

Finally, I also wish to thank Patricia Welbourn Lorsch, my wife, for her help in titling the book and for her love and moral support throughout this process.

Without this village of people the book would not have appeared and I am indebted to all of them. Nonetheless, I take full responsibility for any errors or commission or omission.

Jay W. Lorsch

Introduction

Problem-Solvers

Listen, observe, test—the three words that guide this book lie at the heart of a powerful method for businesses' transformation. The method has gone by many names over the years. Human relations, organizational behavior, the medical model. Whatever the name, the idea is always the same: not to promulgate some theory about how businesses should function but to take the pulse of a real business, get its case history, diagnose its problems, and solve them.

The medical model is so named because it treats businesses like patients and business consultants like skilled physicians. When a patient visits his doctor, it is not enough that she simply guess what ails him by consulting statistical models. Say you were sitting in an exam room, and before asking you any questions or running any tests, your doctor told you, "So you're X years old and weigh Y pounds and have Z preexisting condition, so I conclude that you have disease A." You'd run screaming and find a better doctor.

Statistical models inform clinical medicine, but any decent physician also listens to her patient, to build a case history. She observes her patient under different situations, if possible, gently pulling a muscle this way or that, listening for the sounds entering her stethoscope first on the chest then on the back. And, understanding that no two patients are identical, a good doctor doesn't just consult averages across populations. She runs tests on the particular patient, sometimes multiple tests or the same test over the course of weeks or months. Only then does that good doctor hazard a diagnosis, much less a prescription or treatment plan.

The same should be true for management consultants and scholars. Unfortunately, though, during the last decades management scholarship has adopted the approach of diagnose first, observe and listen later, if at all. Too many managers and managers-in-training, rather than run screaming, accept this newer approach, with its reliance on quantitative statistics and mathematical modeling, as objective and scientific. And management scholars are hired and promoted for promulgating this approach. An ever-persistent difficulty, however, arises that encourages managers and scholars to question the path they've followed in these same decades: management and organizational problems are not getting solved, they are proliferating. We are overdue to revisit the earlier medical model, understand its origin story, identify its uniquely efficacious attributes, and consider how it can offer solutions to both organizations and the training of the next generation of managers and scholars. Boiled down, my argument is that today's management scholars need to think less like theorizing quants and more like observant doctors, just as they did at the dawn of the business school curriculum.

Today the field of management studies is in a state of crisis. After the success of the whiz-kids—originally number-crunchers at the Department of Defense who helped to win the Second World War—gave a newfound caché to quantitative social science, academia in the second half of the 20th century moved in new, supposedly more rigorous directions. While some at the Harvard Business School (HBS)—myself included—carried the torch for human relations and the medical model, business schools overwhelmingly became havens of economists, game theorists, and other calculators of abstraction.

As a result, business schools have ceased to think very much about real businesses, real problems, and real problem-solving. The profession of business academia is larger than ever—the Academy of Management boasted 20,000 members at last count—yet it is irrelevant to real businesses. Most business scholars have nothing to say about why organizations and the people within them behave the way they do. Instead of talking with managers and workers and assembling data on the basis of real findings, business academics defend complex theories about how businesses ought to work and make predictions about what should happen to businesses that follow one or another ideal scheme. Thousands of business professionals still read *Management and the Worker*, F. J. Roethlisberger's 1939 comprehensive and indispensable account of the Hawthorne Study and the human relations idea. No one reads the impenetrable, jargon- and equation-laden journal articles produced by business academics, except other business academics. Instead of creating knowledge and ideas useful to organizations, business scholars pursue academic careerism.

Even the new field of behavioral economics, whose earliest practitioners are garnering Nobel Prizes, whose scholars and popularizers are publishing bestsellers, and whose practices organizations, from companies to governments, are applying with some beneficial consequences—none more remarked on than individuals increasing what they save for retirement—is not entirely free from this fault. Because of my decades spent as a scholar of organizational behavior and as a consultant who has applied my scholarship toward solving organizational problems, I can applaud what behavioral economics shares with my field and lament what it doesn't. With their reliance on presumptive universal biases and cognitive quirks, and their preference for nonreal world controlled experiments, behavioral economists are the lab technicians to the organizational behaviorists' on-call physicians. It is a difference with a history and has quite real consequences for the field of business management.

I believe that the human relations model born a hundred years ago can be a beacon in the field's current moment of crisis. The old, quaint idea of paying attention to what's really going on—to the "phenomena," as the HBS pioneers, discussed in this book, and their followers were known to say—can do very useful things for businesses today and can help us break new academic ground. And, more importantly, we can still use the medical model to solve real problems. Problems of business and, relatedly, problems of society.

Ideally, business consulting and business scholarship, which have been my professions for more than five decades, should look much the same way as our doctor's examination of her patient. The skilled consultant will listen carefully to managers and workers at the organization he has been brought in to help. After all, while top-level decision makers hire consultants, it is often their subordinates who reveal the most about an organization's function and dysfunction. As Paul Lawrence, one of my mentors at HBS, put it, "Our subjects can tell us what needs to be studied."[1] A good consultant asks judicious questions designed to elicit honest, forthright information and to reveal what the consultant does not already know. But he also sits back and watches, taking notes of day-to-day life in the organization, seeking patterns from which to draw empirically sound conclusions. When he believes he understands what may be ailing the organization, he may develop experiments in order to test his understanding and possible remedies. The hallmarks of the medical model—the clinical imperatives of listen, observe, test—are at the center of the field of organizational behavior as it has been taught at HBS through the decades, and it is this method I believe we should return to.

Much like the society of the early 20th century to whose ills the original HBS pioneers responded, our own is in the midst of profound transformations. Just as that first cohort of HBS scholars confronted systemic problems, which included then prevalent and counterproductive management practices, such as Frederick Taylor's scientific management, so too do today's managers and scholars face a world transformed. These transformations have deep roots—in the stagflation and recession of the 1970s, the frenzy of corporate restructuring that followed, and the dissolution of the social contract that had powered the New Deal. The rise of the global corporation and evolution of a postindustrial (and now even a postcorporate) economy have further destabilized our social–political systems. We are now in an era of intense disruption and rapid technological advancement, including the proliferation of robotics and artificial intelligence, which have already fostered significant changes in how people work, and which portend yet greater shifts.

To an extent, labor is being further automated, but there is more to the story. Technology is also re-Taylorizing work and introducing new kinds of precarity. A large proportion of the workforce is now engaged in temporary and contract labor governed through digital platforms. While these new patterns of work have provided fantastic freedom and opportunity for some, many more have found themselves yearning for the certainty of a steady paycheck and benefits and resenting being bossed around by a computer that is precisely calculating every wasted moment.

There is no better time, then, to return to the medical model and learn from the wisdom of its founders, and from some of their later disciples who have used the regime of listen, observe, test to elucidate and solve contemporary business problems. In the pages that follow, I will take the reader back to the origins of the medical model. We will together explore the intellectual developments that undergirded human relations. We will trace the unfortunate eclipse of problem-solving by abstract theory, even as problem-solving continued to generate practical successes while theory merely alienated business scholarship from business. And we will glimpse all that the medical model still offers today.

Where We've Been, Where We're Going

Our story begins in the 1920s, when Wallace Donham took the helm as the second dean of HBS, in pursuit of a decidedly social mission: using scrupulous research to solve business problems, which he saw as essential to the public good. To this end, he assembled new programs at HBS and brought together a diverse faculty interested in applying scientific methods to the problems of business. Chapter 1 explores the early evolution of the medical model, as its intellectually adventurous founders developed connections across disciplines including biology, medicine, sociology, anthropology, and psychology.

Chapter 2 turns in detail to the Hawthorne study, showing how the project progressed under the care of Elton Mayo and Fritz Roethlisberger, two of the faculty members brought together by Donham. In the years that followed, Hawthorne lingered in the minds of researchers and practitioners alike, not least because of Roethlisberger's avid promotion of the work at HBS and among business executives. Human relations became the preeminent paradigm for business research, with HBS in the vanguard and Roethlisberger at the helm. Chapter 2 concludes with a review of the enduring importance of the Hawthorne Study, visible in the work of a later generation of practitioners and scholars that included William Dickson and George Homans.

Chapter 3 turns to some other notable successes of the human relations paradigm in the wake of Hawthorne. One, the Dashman Study, is an HBS case study focused on a real business facing problems that defied management theory. In this instance, a new executive tried to implement promising reforms in his department, only to find them ignored. Theory tells us that businesses operate rationally, so there should be no opposition to wise, reasonable structures and protocols. But observation of the workplace clarified what was really going on and led to new, actionable knowledge—a walking stick. We will also examine Art Turner and

Paul Lawrence's work looking at job satisfaction and my own early work looking at how companies in the plastic industry coordinated major functional units within their businesses. From there we will turn finally to a consideration of *contingency theory*, the theory developed by Paul Lawrence and myself to explain why different companies used different mechanisms for functional integration based on the tasks their companies need to perform.

Chapter 4 hones in on the work of younger colleagues such as John Kotter, Jack Gabarro, and Linda Hill and my own research into management problems in white-collar workplaces. It traces the evolution of, and with that evolution the continued usefulness of, the medical model across generations and domains of study. From a still famed and often referred to study of a General Foods pet food factory in Topeka, Kansas, to Kotter's interest in city mayors during the 1970s to the more recent work of Linda Hill and John "Jack" Gabarro, the refinement of the medical model allows for, and I will argue aligns with, a practice of testing the findings of research gathered by adhering to the HBS founders' invention of "walking sticks," real-world data gathering.

Chapter 5 discusses the state of the field today and emphasizes how much has changed in business education and scholarship since the heyday of the medical model. It considers my own work on boards of directors, David Thomas and Jack Gabarro's work on the challenges facing African American executives who reached upper levels of management and the factors that enabled them to rise. It also looks at Tsedal Neeley's work on the effects of English as a lingua franca in the Japanese global company, Rakuten. This chapter also looks though at how and why our field has been eclipsed by the quants and gives some examples of what I think are the problems resulting from this eclipse.

In my conclusion, I ask how business research can escape the unfortunate corner into which it has been drawn, where it has become an ivory tower convention. Most of it has nothing to do with business practice, let alone our many urgent social problems. Where there is some discernible connection to business, the research results are too obscure to make sense of or to furnish a plan of action. Though there are a few practitioners of the medical method out there today, business scholarship is, on the whole, irrelevant to real business. My final question in this book: how can our field regain relevance and have social impact at a time of urgent need?

My answer will be obvious by now: listen, observe, test. Improve practice through engagement with the realities of the factory floor and the executive suite and everything in between. Recognize that an organization is not only its balance sheets and bottom lines but also its people. And those people do not exist only within the boundaries of an organization. The lives we lead inside and outside of work are intimately connected and tie the functioning of organizations to the functioning of society itself. Analysis that relies entirely on numbers, or that fails to account for broader context, is leaving out too much. To quote an old saw, "Not everything that can be counted counts, and not everything that counts can be counted."

The medical model still works. It works across industries and management contexts. It works because it is not a theory. Theories in the social sciences always fail in the specific instance because no theory can adequately account for every variable of our complex human lives and interactions. Instead, what is useful to managers is a framework for thinking about problems of the here-and-now and for addressing them with practical solutions. The medical model provides such a framework. It is not totally innocent of theory, but only inasmuch as it relies on the very basic and incontestable presumption that organizations are made of people and that people are complicated but knowable. From this humble foundation, the medical model offers powerful tools for anyone looking to solve organization problems and get things done.

CHAPTER 1

In and Out of the Laboratory

In 1919, Wallace Donham took over the helm of HBS as its second dean. Under his leadership a new, human-centric approach to solving the problems of business was developed, the medical method or the "human relations model" as it was also called, in hopes of solving the ever larger problems of a postwar, industrial society experiencing rapid and fundamental change. Donham brought together at HBS a collection of new thinkers with different backgrounds; men such as Lawrence Henderson, Elton Mayo, and Fritz Roethlisberger. Each man had different specialties. Henderson was a biologist and an MD, whose fascination with anthropology and the nascent field of sociology led him to apply his knowledge of anatomy to social systems. Mayo was a clinical psychologist, skilled in asking troubled people the kinds of questions that would reveal the roots of their problems. And Roethlisberger was their chief acolyte and popularizer. Together, Mayo and Roethlisberger applied Henderson's ideas in practical circumstances, showing how intellectual thoughts about the man (or woman) in the organization could actually solve real problems on the factory floor.

It is hard to overstate just how unorthodox the human relations model was in those days. (Human relations was the founders' preferred term.) The longstanding assumption had been that organizations were essentially hydraulic systems prone to breakdown. Managers greased gears and tightened screws in hopes that the machine would keep chugging along. In less metaphorical terms, working a factory job, say, was presumed to be inherently unpleasant, so the manager's job was to figure out how to efficiently extract labor from the reluctant worker through wage incentives, control, and punishment.

The human relations perspective, in contrast, conceived of work not as a hydraulic system but as a social one. Workers within organizations have complex economic and psychological needs. These needs overlap within the workplace, and they escape the workplace: workers' lives matter to their productivity. Elton Mayo pointed to this "intricate web of human relations"[1] and called on management to serve as its "chief maintainer, balancer, and facilitator."[2] Though today we are apt to hear intrusively paternalistic presumptions in Mayo's declaration, and unquestionably human relations pioneers of the early 20th century were products of their own times, we should also acknowledge that in seeing workers as humans, and not machines for control and punishment, Mayo *et al.* took giant progressive steps forward. That tradition, and not the hidebound era in which it arose, is what today we can applaud.

Whereas in the earlier conception of work and organizations the manager's tools were wages and supervision, in this new conception the manager was asked to create an environment in which employees felt they could "belong and grow" as well as contribute and cooperate. Although this perspective challenged decades of managerial theory, it was in some ways perfectly obvious. So believed Fritz Roethlisberger, to whom the human relations approach "merely mean[t] that, in the last analysis, business is an organization of people."[3]

Until this time, no one had thought very hard about the human element in business. It is no wonder that the early 20th century brought the height of labor unrest. The Industrial Revolution had brought about massive advances in communication, automation, and production, in the process radically altering both the environment and function of the worker. In a relatively short period of time, urban workers left behind small, often family-owned, workshops to take up unskilled labor in massive factories where they were subject to policies and punishments handed down from executives they rarely saw. The introduction of the assembly line and strict output quotas stripped work of its traditional meaning, leaving workers angry and disoriented and fueling waves of complaint and even violence—not to mention unionization and the emergence of a prolabor politics that had the potential to threaten bottom lines. Yet executives and industrial engineers were blind to the sources of the seething discontent.

The problem was that executives thought about numbers, not people. Sure, they could agree that the assembly line was boring, but thanks to modern technology and logistics, goods were cheap. So cheap that the average worker at the plant could afford them. If everyone was making enough money, what was the problem? Rather than ask why workers resisted the assembly line so fiercely, management doubled down. They turned to Frederick Taylor and other prophets of scientific management—so-called Taylorism—who claimed that restive workers could be manipulated into compliance through the optimization of payment-output schemes. The human factor—the emotional and social consequences of a rapidly changing industrial environment—had no place here. Henderson and Mayo, however, saw the parallels between understanding human illness and diagnosing organizational dysfunctions, rooted in a deep understanding of the "presenting symptoms." They discovered that a clinical, or systems, approach is the most reliable way to enhance our understanding of complex organizations.

In 1927, Lawrence Henderson launched a curious project in the basement of HBS's newly constructed Morgan Hall. Curious, because the project hardly seemed like the kind one would expect in a business school. The effort was called the "Fatigue Laboratory," and the goal was to investigate the physiological effects of the industrial environment—research that intended to address problems critical both for individual workers and for society at large. "During the past two centuries, and especially within 50 years, the social environment of man has suffered a change for which there is no parallel," Henderson wrote. "The effect of this revolution upon present economic, social, and individual situations is but little known, though it is amply attested to by the amount of mental disorder, industrial upheaval, and international trouble of our time."[4]

The revolution Henderson had in mind was of course the Industrial Revolution, which by the 1920s had long since transformed business globally. Innovations in steel, electricity, and petroleum enabled the expansion of transportation systems and the concurrent establishment of extensive telecommunication networks, creating a national market in the United States. For the first time in history, a producer in Iowa could compete for market share from New Jersey to New Mexico. These developments spawned the advent of mass production, as companies sought to drive down costs and increase production capacity to take advantage of newly available mass-distribution schemes and the competitive opportunities that accompanied them. The creation of sprawling factories in combination with novel machinery allowed manufacturers to produce far more for far less money. By the early 20th century, most consumer goods in American households came from mass producers rather than home-makers or local artisans.

Business at speed and scale necessitated new approaches to work. In particular, large companies required complex administration to coordinate and control operational demands. The number of trained, salaried managers exploded during this period, and business evolved from a trade to a profession with journals, associations, and graduate education programs. And because firms were now competing for the same national market rather than for local customers, managers faced intense pressure to optimize results. They constantly looked for ways to squeeze additional productive capacity not only out of their physical plant but also out of their human capital. Workers, it was believed, were not so unlike the factory machines.

This was the birth of "scientific management," which extended the logics of rationalization and efficiency to the worker.[5] Frederick Taylor, scientific management's most prominent figure, compared management to physics or chemistry, suggesting that, like these disciplines, management dealt in physical constants. "The best management is a true science, resting upon clearly defined laws, rules, and principles," he asserted; a manager had only to discover the "one best way."[6] To this end, he famously roamed factory floors with his stopwatch, timing and measuring output so as to design tasks for optimal efficiency. Two of Taylor's disciples, Frank and Lilian Gilbreth, pursued the same agenda by using new photographic reduction technology to study the micromovements of workers.[7] Workers, who were believed to be naturally lazy and prone to "soldiering," could also be optimized through sophisticated incentive and surveillance systems. "Work consists mainly of simple, not particularly interesting, tasks," Taylor famously claimed, "The only way to get people to do them is to incentivize them properly and monitor them carefully."

Systems of scientific management were put into practice in factories across the country, fundamentally altering the structure and texture of work. Unsurprisingly, workers were less than enthusiastic about their new conditions. Mass manufacturing factories employed tens of thousands of workers, including women and children. Work in these factories was often characterized by grueling, monotonous jobs. Fourteen-hour days were not uncommon. It is easily forgotten that before this time, human beings had lived not according to the clock, but to the sun and the season. The Fatigue Lab was an effort to understand what effect scientific management had on the men and women subject to it. Biology, Henderson reasoned, was a logical place to start looking for these effects, as the modern factory setting represented a major shift in the physical environment of people's lives. "The activities of their muscles, their postures, and their mental processes, are all more or less modified, and nothing or next to nothing is known about these things," Henderson wrote.[8]

The Fatigue Lab undertook a variety of innovative, sometimes unorthodox, experiments to test the effects of various industrial conditions on the human biological system. On the more prosaic side, the lab dispatched researchers to factories to assess the blood pressure of workers as they toiled. Volunteers, including MBA students and soldiers from Fort Devens—as well as dogs, who did not volunteer—were monitored while running on treadmills. Henderson investigated the human body's ability to adapt to extreme conditions of heat and cold and to the effects of high altitude. Lab documents show an order for "six alligators 24 – 36 inches long," for what purpose one can only imagine.[9]

A World of Change and Difficulty

To understand the world of difficulties that Henderson sought to address, we need to look back at what industry meant in the early twentieth century—what it accomplished, how it was perceived, and what deleterious consequences it sometimes had for workers.

In 1904, the Ford Motor Company was a small, artisanal business. Skilled machinists working in teams assembled individual automobiles from start to finish in a process that was both arduous and artful. That year, Ford produced and sold 1,745 Model Bs, each priced at $2,000. Then, in 1910, Ford moved production into a much larger facility on a 60-acre plot in Highland Park, Michigan. The factory had been designed to accommodate an assembly line, an entirely new approach to manufacturing. The industrial engineers who devised the assembly line expected it to be able to complete a new vehicle, the Model T, every 40 seconds. And so it did. In 1916, three years after the first assembly line was installed, the company sold 577,036 Model Ts, each for $360.[10]

The Highland Park assembly line aroused both awe and anger. A true technological feat, the line brought the work to the worker, rather than the other way around. And the volume and price of the output was astonishing. Once luxuries for the super-rich, automobiles were suddenly available to the middle class, a group that was burgeoning, thanks to plentiful factory jobs. But the workers themselves were not so much impressed with the technological novelty and low prices as they were concerned about the prospect of endless hours of depersonalized, monotonous labor. Historian David A. Hounshell describes the scene:

> No longer did the men stand at individual workbenches, each putting together an entire flywheel magneto assembly from the many parts.... This was no April Fool's joke. The workers had been instructed by the foreman to place one particular part in the assembly or perhaps start a few nuts or even just tighten them and then push the flywheel down the row to the next worker. Having pushed it down eighteen or perhaps thirty-six inches, the workers repeated the same process, over and over, nine hours, over and over.[11]

As the Ford Motor Company continued to grow, making cars ever more available and affordable for the American masses, the workers in the Ford factory became increasingly disgruntled. By the end of the first year of assembly line production, the factory had extremely high rates of labor turnover. Keith Sward, author of *The Legend of Henry Ford*, writes, "So great was labor's distaste for the new machine system that toward the close of 1913 every time the company wanted to add 100 men to its factory personnel, it was necessary to hire 963."[12] The wife of one assembly line worker wrote to Henry Ford in 1914, "The chain system you have is a slave driver! My God! Mr. Ford. My husband has come home & thrown himself down and won't eat his supper—so done out! Can't it be remedied?"[13] Ford offered a wage increase of five dollars per day to assuage labor unrest, but the pay raise was more strategic than humanitarian. It was meant, Hounsell writes, to ensure that "the essential human appendages to this machine would always be present."[14]

The period was also marked by rising economic inequality, which peaked in 1928—a record not broken until the present day. The spectacular wealth generated by industrial advancement went overwhelmingly into the pockets of the managerial class, while many workers toiled for less than a living wage. Those with any regular wage, however, considered themselves lucky: day labor was a highly uncertain gig, leaving Americans routinely without income. Safety was another serious issue. As early as 1915, the Bureau of Labor Statistics estimated the number of on-the-job deaths at 35,000, many of them preventable.[15]

Resistance—to low wages; to managerial control; to indecent, unsafe, and excessively tiring working conditions—emerged in the political arena, in the forms of the Populist Party and the Progressive Movement. And alongside political agitation came labor unrest, which rose in frequency and intensity. Worker sabotage, absenteeism, and strikes characterized the labor relations of the early 20th century and presented a mounting challenge for managers, many of whom could not understand the source of this discontent. After all, mass production had made accessible and affordable items previously available only to the wealthy. Certainly, this meant that work was more monotonous, less autonomous, and took more time, but what a small price to pay for a tin lizzie in every driveway!

Yet labor dissatisfaction continued to grow ever more disruptive and violent. Between 1881 and 1885, the United States averaged 528 strikes per year, with 176,511 workers involved annually. From 1916 to 1918, the average rose to 3,864 strikes per year with nearly 1.4 million workers involved. With the establishment of trade unions such as the International Workers of the World, founded in 1904, strikes became not only more frequent but better organized. By 1910 trade union membership was 2.1 million, accounting for about 10 percent of all wage earners; 10 years later, membership had more than doubled to almost 4.9 million, nearly 20 percent of the labor force.[16] These strikes were hugely costly to companies and generated bad press, public outcry, and considerable harm when they turned violent.

A case in point is the 1909 labor action at the Pressed Steel Car (PSC) Company in McKees Rocks, Pennsylvania. PSC, a leading manufacturer that employed thousands of men, was notorious for poor relations between management and workers. One anonymous journalist writing for *American Manufacturer and Iron World* suggested that if officials would start treating laborers as human beings rather than "chattels," the company as a whole might fare far better.[17]

A major problem was the company's decision, eight years previously, to employ the principles of Taylor's scientific management, instituting an assembly line production system with by-unit pay to incentivize workers to increase their individual output. But this system only served to aggravate hostility between native-born skilled workers—who did not do piecework and therefore did not benefit from this new pay scheme and continued to earn about $10 to $15 per week—and foreign-born unskilled workers, who could now earn up to $25 per week. In response to the tensions, management shifted to a wage-pooling system, but that scheme also resulted in significant friction among workers, as slower colleagues, the mistakes of another gang, or the decisions of foremen could hold down the wages of faster and more effective workers.[18]

On July 13, 1909, over 3,000 men, unhappy with the wage system and with management's refusal to listen to their continuing grievances, walked off their jobs. This form of sabotage was one of labor's only weapons, but by this point employers had learned they could respond by hiring scabs. The management at McKees Rocks did just this, applying further pressure on striking workers by evicting them from company housing and sending a private police force after them. By late August, the protests had turned to deadly riots, with a series of gun battles between strikers and police leaving six dead and at least 36 people injured, some seriously.[19] Ultimately, the strike ended when labor representatives reached an agreement with company management, but the resolution was a pyrrhic victory: the workers received no wage increases, only a promise from the company that workmen could expect to "share the benefits" as business conditions improved.[20]

The strike at McKees Rocks underscores the multiple, deeply rooted causes of industrial unrest in this period of profound disruption—changing organizational structure and power hierarchies, monotonous tasks and long work hours in dismal conditions, wage dissatisfaction, and employers' perceived or actual lack of respect for and understanding of their employees. McKees Rocks was also an early sign that scientific management, with its emphasis on financial incentives, was ineffective in curtailing worker unrest and improving efficiency and productivity. New ideas were needed, and the first business schools emerged around this time with the goal of providing them.

Pioneers

HBS was founded in 1908 with the goal of professionalizing business administration by introducing to that career certain principles and ideals akin to those governing the practices of law and medicine. Edwin Gay, the first dean of HBS, believed that the new institution could shape the world of business by instilling in its students "a habit of intellectual respect for business as a profession."[21] But Gay had something else in mind, too. Nodding to the discontent of the period, he also believed that HBS's students should graduate with a sense of the "social implications" of their work "and the heightened sense of responsibility which goes with that."[22]

It was Wallace Donham, however, who provided the truly revolutionary vision for business education that began to take shape at Harvard. Donham assumed his position in 1919, a time of institutional transition when a strategic thinker could reimagine what the young school might become. After all, the First World War had left HBS essentially dormant; in 1919, the school graduated only four students. But the next fall, enrollment numbered 422, mostly veterans. In addition to stabilizing the size of the student body, Donham had to attract talented faculty and oversee the construction of a new campus in Boston, across the Charles River from Cambridge and Harvard Yard.

Donham, himself a Harvard graduate, had a successful career as a banker and lawyer for the Old Colony Trust Bank of Boston. But he was coaxed back to academia by the opportunity to pursue lofty aims for the business school, arguing that the "development, strengthening, and multiplication of socially minded businessmen is the central problem of business."[23] His perspective was influenced by his experience as a court-ordered receiver for the Bay State Railway, where he had resolved strikes so successfully that the union gave him an award. From his personal interactions with workers, Donham concluded that the ability to comprehend the complexity of human behavior was fundamental to the profession of business. The "labor problem," Donham believed, required the development of "far more knowledge and consideration for human nature and of the physiological and psychological bases for the actions of men."[24]

And if Donham had a history with worker unrest, he also was a keen observer of the rapid change afoot in the larger industrial environment. "Discontent with the existing condition of things is perhaps more wide-spread than ever before in history," he wrote. "These conditions are trans-forming the world simultaneously for better and for worse. They compel a complete reappraisal of the significance of business."[25] The innovations that had enabled mass production had been implemented, Donham felt, without due attention to their human and social impact. "We have yet to learn how to deal with these revolutionary consequences of science," Donham cautioned, adding that

> The greatest portion of this responsibility falls ... on the business group, for businessmen have the effective control over the mecha-nisms produced by science and therefore responsibility for ... the working out of these new problems.[26]

In a period when businessmen and scientific managers were obsessed with productivity and efficiency, Donham broke with orthodoxy by seek-ing to infuse an ethics of responsibility into business training. With this in mind, he sought to develop a research program that would generate knowledge of the human aspects of business, which in 1920 had been little remarked on. He would need collaborators, scholars who shared his concerns and were creative enough to do what had not been done before. So it was that Donham enlisted the help of his former college classmate, Lawrence J. Henderson.

Henderson's path to the study of human behavior in business did not follow a straight line. After graduating from Harvard College, where he majored in chemistry, Henderson went on to get his MD at Harvard Medical School. While he had no intention of becoming a practicing physician, he was interested in Harvard's medical curriculum because it offered a good introduction to human biology and was steeped in scientific methods and the Hippocratic Oath: "First, do no harm." Henderson became a biomedical researcher, and early in his career made a name for himself by establishing the normal pH of human blood (7.4) and developing the Henderson–Hasselbalch equation, which expresses the mathematical relationship of the blood's carbon dioxide, bicarbonate, and hydrogen ions—a formula used to determine changes in acid–base balance under various conditions. The equation is an elegant statement of an organism's response to its environment, and Henderson's publications from this period—*The Fitness of the Environment* (1913), *The Order of Nature* (1925), and *Blood: A Study in General Physiology* (1928)—all reflect his interest in biological adaptation to external influences—precisely the sort of thing he studied at the Fatigue Lab.

Early on in his tenure as dean, Donham began talking with his old classmate about the future of business education and what it could contribute, given the industrial conditions of the time.[27] Through these informal conversations, the two men discovered their shared concern for the "neglect" by both businessmen and scientists of the pressing human problems of modern society. Yet Henderson agreed that business education could make a difference, particularly in improving the lot of workers. "Here, it seems to me, is one of the great opportunities for advances in understanding the problems of labor," Henderson announced in a 1927 speech:

> It is an opportunity which the business schools should seize, to the end that they may grow in understanding of what the men who study in the business schools are really going to do when they pass out into the world and begin to control the lives of others.[28]

Moving from natural to social science was a challenge for Henderson. In his early career, he seemed to believe that human behavior, in all its nonrational complexity, should be the purview of the arts, not the sciences.[29] But what bridged the natural and social sciences was the idea of systems. As the historian Crane Brinton, who was at one time a student of Henderson's, recalled, Henderson's passion became "the study of the organization of systems" whether they be "in nature or in life."[30]

In his work as a biochemist, Henderson elucidated the relationships among multiple factors in the blood, a project that understood blood as a complex system with interacting components that had to be balanced so that the whole system—that is, blood—could function. He came to see organizations similarly. Systems were "useful despite the fact that [they were] a creation of the imagination. Systems imposed boundaries and mapped out relationships: within them, facts made sense. They were ordered and interrelated. They became amenable to logical consideration."[31] Understanding the properties of systems and the dynamic relationship between internal and external environments remained consistent themes of Henderson's work, even as he moved from blood chemistry to social dynamics.

As Henderson's interests broadened from biology into the social sphere, he yearned for a systemic way of thinking about human psychology and society but knew of no conceptual framework for the social sciences that equaled the rigorous systematic thinking of the natural sciences. That is, until William Morton Wheeler, an entomologist at Harvard with an interest in the social systems of insects, introduced Henderson to the sociology of Vilfredo Pareto.[32] Pareto offered Henderson exactly what he had been looking for. As Roethlisberger later described it, "Up to this time Henderson had shared the disdain that most members of the harder sciences have for the softer ones ..., however, when Henderson discovered Pareto, he became a one-book sociologist."[33]

Pareto, a fellow intellectual wanderer, began his academic career with a dissertation on "The Equilibrium of Solid Bodies." This early interest in the adaptive abilities of natural systems foreshadowed a lifelong preoccupation with systems analysis and equilibrium, spanning the physical, economic, and social realms (sound familiar?). Pareto's work was always inductive and empirical.[34]

Over the course of his career, Pareto grew increasingly aware of the central role of the "sentiments," as he called them, in understanding human activity and society. He committed himself to creating an intellectual framework that could treat the nonlogical elements of society with a high level of rigor. In a speech at the University of Lausanne, he emphasized the value of applying experimental research to the study of the sentiments and searching for "the similarities presented by social phenomena: they will teach us about the facts and about the relationships of the facts."[35] He also pointed to "the mutual dependence of social phenomena" as a chief obstacle to fully understanding human activity.[36]

Pareto's work was radical both in its audacious confrontation of nonlogical human behavior and in its novel application of scientific investigative methodology to the study of society. In a process not unlike biological taxonomy, Pareto set out to break down observable human behaviors and expressions of sentiments into their smallest components and then to search for unifying patterns among those parts. He then applied this view to society as a whole, hypothesizing that society relied upon a shared system of sentiments and "derivations"—justifications for action. Just as humans attempted to maintain equilibrium between sentiments and reasons, so did society, Pareto thought. Societal equilibrium was maintained by the constant adjustment of sentiments and justifications in reaction to any disturbance. Inspired by Pareto, Henderson saw that it was possible to identify systematic properties—such as the mutual dependence of variables in the system—in social phenomena, not just in biological ones.

While Henderson was uninterested in much of the abstract theory that dominated sociology in his day, he saw Pareto's sociology as a useful tool for "continuous, persistent occupation with a subject" through sensory observation.[37] Indeed, he likened Pareto's approach to the Hippocratic method in medicine, which emphasizes, above all else, the importance of gaining intimate knowledge of a subject through extended practice. Only by gaining the intuitive familiarity accessed through "hard, persistent, intelligent, responsible, unremitting labor in the sick room, not in the library,"[38] could one begin to observe accurately the patterns, recurrences, and relationships among observable facts—the patterns that constitute systematic knowledge. By building up systematic knowledge through skilled observation, one could slowly, cautiously, begin to construct a conceptual framework about the phenomena. That framework could then be used as an investigative tool to make better observations and interpretations about a wide range of social phenomena.

Henderson called this kind of tool a "walking stick." It was an essential and defining characteristic, one that figuratively underscored the importance of scholars and managers leaving the lab and entering the real world. He rejected philosophic theory, which tried to explain phenomena, but was amenable to "a useful walking stick to help on the way" to understanding.[39] As Roethlisberger later explained it, the function of walking sticks—he and colleagues also used the term "conceptual schemes"—"is not to explain but to fix attention upon what is to be first observed and in time explained. Their attributes are utility and convenience for purposes of investigation, not truth or falsity or clarity for purposes of explanation."[40]

While Henderson was elaborating his understanding of social systems in hopes of addressing the problems of modern labor, he came upon the work of a man who would become a key collaborator: Elton Mayo. A clinical psychologist at the University of Queensland in Brisbane, Australia, Mayo, too, was concerned about the social problems of the moment. And, like Henderson, he sought to apply his disciplinary knowledge in new realms. Mayo had originally pursued a career as a physician, but after dropping out of medical school twice, he had moved to London to teach at Working Men's College. This experience exposed him to the social problems of the new industrial environment and motivated him to study psychology. He saw in the wide-ranging principles of New Psychology—propounded by the likes of Pierre Janet, Sigmund Freud, Alfred Adler, and Carl Jung—keys to solving social problems. What unified these thinkers, if little else, was the shared belief that psychological character is shaped by biology and early interpersonal experiences, especially in the family. Mayo would come to believe that interpersonal relationships were essential factors in work performance, an idea that had never previously been explored systematically.

In a 1919 lecture, Mayo passionately denounced the tendency of industrial leaders to "ignore the human elements in work" and to employ methods that "provoke destructive impulses" in the worker.[41] He spoke about the desperate need for psychological research into industrial unrest, which could only be done effectively in the environment of work itself. But mounting administrative duties at the University of Queensland prevented Mayo from pursuing his calling, so he decided to seek a new post. The United States seemed to provide better opportunities for the research he had in mind, and after a 1923 visit he began scoping out factory sites and sources of funding. He found an early home at the University of Pennsylvania's Wharton School of Commerce and Finance.[42]

Mayo conducted his first stateside research at Philadelphia textile mills experiencing exceptionally high employee turnover. Amid the racket of the factory's engine rooms, Mayo talked with workers and listened to their stories. What he heard reminded him of his experiences back home with shell-shocked soldiers returning from Europe. He noticed that, in the case of soldiers and workers alike, hostile conditions provoked obsessive thinking—"reverie," as he called it. And industrial laborers in particular suffered from a dreadful monotony that led to "irritability, depression, and other irrationalities."[43]

Donham and Henderson were both impressed by Mayo's forays into industrial psychology, and, after delivering an invited lecture at Harvard, Mayo was offered a post at HBS. Mayo and Henderson made a bit of an odd couple. Henderson was abrasive and imposing, with a fiery red beard that earned him the nicknames "Pink Whiskers" and "Jesus" among his students. Mayo, on the other hand, was physically slight, with a bald head and glaucoma. To protect his eyes, he would smoke his cigarettes out of a long holder of interlocking goose quills.[44] A famously able conversationalist and inspiring teacher, Mayo made an ideal guest at dinner parties, and loved to entertain the table with stories and humorous takes on current events. Henderson was also an old hand in Boston's medical circles, while Mayo was a newcomer—a distinction that mattered more than it should have.

Despite their differences, Mayo and Henderson developed a bond that was both personally intimate and intellectually productive. The two men treated each other with immense respect, somewhat of a rarity for Henderson. They were both, as Roethlisberger put it, "adventurers in the realm of ideas" who tended to follow their wide-ranging academic interests with a disregard for disciplinary boundaries.[45] They also shared an interest in applying scientific methods of observation and analysis to the study of social phenomena, believing that "only this approach ... would raise psychological and sociological work from sentimental, biased, and philosophic inexactitudes to the level of a respected science."[46]

And Mayo would do precisely this, albeit the path was not an easy one. While Henderson's Fatigue Lab got off to a fast start, Mayo's part of the HBS research program, the newly established Department of

Industrial Relations, struggled to get off the ground. Mayo was the only member of the department who had any experience in the field, so he trained students and colleagues in psychological methods such as interviewing. Establishing an independent line of investigation presented problems and initially the Industrial Research Department worked in tandem with the Fatigue Lab. One obstacle was finding a research site. Another was deciding what data to gather and what methods should be used to collect it—interviewing workers, of course, but what exactly should they be asked? How to give them the opportunity to speak their minds, yet also elicit information that could be quantified without sacrificing its core meaning? The contrast between Henderson's and Mayo's efforts seemed very great. As Roethlisberger put it, describing his own early experiences at HBS:

> What Henderson and the Fatigue Laboratory would do Monday morning at 9 a.m. was clearer to me than what Mayo would be up to. Henderson and his colleagues … could set up their treadmills, and they could measure the physiological effects (on dogs and men) of different simulated conditions of work. Mayo, on the other hand, seemed to be sitting in his office and practicing his charisma or doing his research on me.[47]

While the Fatigue Lab benefited from the well-established methods and approaches of the biological sciences, the framework for Mayo's field research was less clear. In essence, Mayo and his young colleagues were tasked with building a new science of industrial psychology from the ground up. To this end, they thought a lot about what kind of scholars they *did not* want to be: the kind with "little first-hand acquaintance," who "preferred to indulge in large abstractions, noble sentiments, or great affairs" and whose "theories were not relevant to concrete practice."[48] That is, what one might call "armchair academics," researchers who never left the library or the faculty lounge.

At the same time, the Industrial Relations group gradually developed a repertoire of concepts and approaches that they felt were indeed useful in studying and analyzing concrete social and psychological phenomena, a prism through which they could view industrial organizations and the people who worked in them. The sociologist Emile Durkheim appealed because of his notion that society could not be measured by the sum of its parts but rather represented a complex equilibrium that, if disrupted, would lead to social disorder—exactly the situation the late Industrial Revolution epitomized. The group generally rejected two other prominent sociologists, Karl Marx and Max Weber, because their theories offered narrowly rationalistic interpretations of human organizations, leaving out the emotional elements of behavior.

Alongside Durkheim, another major influence proved to be the anthropologist Bronislaw Malinowski, whose model of social anthropology emphasized intensive fieldwork and rich narrative. In Malinowski's most famous study, among Trobriand Islanders, he departed from traditional scholarly practice by participating in the activities of the island and forming social relationships with the people there.[49] Malinowski was adamant about analyzing human behavior in its context, and so was Mayo. The two of them met in 1914 at the University of Queensland, where Malinowski was visiting on one of his many trips to and from the Trobriands. The two became close friends and mutual admirers. "The real scientific mind is absolutely in touch with life," Malinowski once wrote in a letter to Mayo. "During my wanderings in English-speaking countries I had the privilege of meeting such a mind only once—at a backwater university in subtropical Australia."[50]

Mayo also was inspired by the anthropologist A. B. Radcliffe-Brown, another Durkheimian. Like Malinowski, Radcliffe-Brown conceived of the societies he studied as social systems, but he placed a greater emphasis on the concept of function. As Radcliffe-Brown saw it, following Durkheim, the function of a social institution was "the correspondence between it and the needs of the social organism."[51] By "needs" Radcliffe-Brown meant the "necessary conditions of existence." Thus, he was suggesting that social institutions were not ideal types, their purposes defined and invariant from the start. Rather, institutions had histories, and in the course of these histories, they developed certain utilities to match social needs. In turn, by fulfilling social needs, institutions were woven durably into social structures. The underlying analogy between social and organic life—the "social organism"—no doubt appealed to Henderson as well.[52]

But for Mayo and scholars of industrial relations, studying the literature was of course insufficient. They needed to do on-site research but were frustrated by the lack of opportunities. Several of Mayo's associates had gained entrance into industrial settings for the purposes of the Fatigue Lab's physiological research, but companies were less welcoming of the psychosocial research the Industrial Relations Department hoped to conduct.[53] This disparity irritated Mayo; while physiological research was undoubtedly important, he knew it was only part of the puzzle. Progress could not be made without a thorough investigation into the psychological and social aspects of industrial life. Reflecting his frustration, one day in the spring of 1928, Mayo burst into Donham's office and declared, "I do not dare go on as we are. Too many problems originate in the home or community. We must go into social studies."[54]

Another obstacle was Mayo's relative obscurity in American intellectual circles. His research in Philadelphia had put him in contact with business practitioners, but even after moving to Harvard, his interaction with scholars and university-associated scientists remained limited. Seeking a new perspective, Mayo returned to London in the summer of 1928—his first time back in more than 20 years. The trip proved hugely invigorating, as he renewed his friendship with Malinowski and socialized with prominent European social thinkers, including the British industrial-fatigue researchers Eric Farmer, May Smith, Millias Culpin, and D. R. Wilson. The cross-disciplinary collaboration Mayo observed at the London School of Economics (LSE), where he was an honorary faculty member during his stay, particularly impressed him. LSE had developed "something in the nature of an integrated point of view which persists through all the discussions and differences of various members of the staff," he recounted in a letter to Donham.[55] Mayo went on to explain the importance of such an integrative approach to the study of human behavior:

> The term I have used on occasion to denote this approach to human investigation is "total situation." It is interesting to me that Malinowski, the economists, the French sociologists, are, equally with Dr. Henderson and myself, finding this necessary as an approach to the study of human problems.[56]

Mayo returned to Harvard declaring to Donham that industrial research was, "in its human aspect, ... at the threshold of a new era of understanding and collaboration."[57]

Soon after his return to the United States in fall 1928, Mayo found the research opportunity he had been looking for: he was commissioned by John D. Rockefeller Jr. to investigate labor problems at the Rockefeller-owned Colorado Fuel and Iron Company. The company had been the site of the famous 1914 Ludlow Massacre, a violent conflict between management and workers in the mines and steelworks. At least 19 people were killed, including five miners, two women, and 11 children, slaughtered by company police and the Colorado National Guard in the miners' camps, and one of the attackers.

In the wake of the massacre, Colorado Fuel and Iron instituted an industrial plan in hopes of improving labor relations. For instance, the plan included a new Committee on Conciliation and Wages, which included representatives from both management and workers. However, more than a decade after its inception, the plan had proved a failure. The company brought in two industrial researchers, Benjamin Selekman and Mary van Kleeck, to assess ongoing problems, but their recommendation— increasing democratic participation of workers in management—also did little to ameliorate tensions.

In October 1928, Mayo spent three weeks at the company's plant in Pueblo Colorado, studying workers' "total situation" using clinical interviewing and community-survey techniques.[58] This methodology, which simultaneously attended to both the individual and the wider social context, became the cornerstone of future research by the Harvard human relations group. Mayo's interviews revealed that workers' ingrained distrust of management had led them to resist participating in the original industrial plan. The surveys, meanwhile, uncovered deep disorder in the larger community, including public health concerns, poverty, and depression. Mayo's recommendations to the company were based on "the direct relationship between social organization or disorganization and industrial content or unrest"[59] and suggested that the industrial plan had failed because it had been conceived without an intimate understanding of the specific "human situation" at the plant. "Human relations," he wrote, "is a problem of industry which calls for intelligence and initiative on both sides … one has to discover what the problems are before administering predetermined solutions."[60]

Between Mayo and Henderson, human relations had its intellectual and methodological backbone. Already the program of listen, observe, and test was taking shape. And the researchers were gaining a foothold in industry and with it the opportunity to affect practical decision making. But it would be the last and youngest of our three pioneers, an acolyte and collaborator of the other two, who made human relations a phenomenon and embedded the social side of business deep in the minds of practitioners and academics alike. That man was Fritz J. Roethlisberger.

By the time I arrived at HBS in the early 1960s, Roethlisberger was a living legend. But in the 1920s, he was still fumbling his way along. He had spent the previous decade meandering from one thing to another, never quite achieving what he called "certainty." (Do any of us?) Spurning his family's cheese-making business, he attended Staten Island Academy and then Columbia University. In 1920, he went to MIT to study engineering administration, which turned out to be another term for scientific management. Roethlisberger described his years at MIT as "a steady disillusionment from beginning to end."[61] He found his courses in scientific management, which advocated practices like keeping the toilets hot in summer and cold in winter to discourage employees spending time there, to be "pure, unadulterated nonsense."[62]

After graduation, Roethlisberger gave an engineering career a half-hearted shot, but he soon quit his job analyzing oil samples in Texas. Thereafter he traveled in Mexico, where he worked in sales for a New York publisher. Finally, he enrolled at Harvard to study mathematical philosophy under the great Alfred North Whitehead. But while Whitehead's approach to philosophy suited Roethlisberger's "search for certainty," the young scholar was ambivalent about its "logical austerity." "I was enthralled even though I was chilled to the bone," he wrote.[63] He soon grew disenchanted with the sterile version of truth proffered by abstract mathematical proofs; "I was still an eager beaver in search of the truth in the 'here and now' and not at some place and time in the 'there and then,'" he wrote.[64] He abandoned his dissertation on Descartes—too many books to read, and in French!

But then, as seems to happen when we are at our lowest, a "miracle" occurred. On the advice of an acquaintance, Roethlisberger consulted with Mayo, who had earned a reputation for his skill in counseling MBA students on their personal and psychological troubles. The meeting was part therapy, part job interview. "Mayo turned my attention to all those matters from which I wanted to escape," Roethlisberger explained— those matters of the here and now that meant so little in Whitehead's intellectual universe.

> With this new look at the adult world of which I could make no sense and from whose nonsenses I was desperately trying to run, a new Fritz was born. What had been something from which to escape became now a new source of intense curiosity.[65]

It was Roethlisberger's closest taste of certainty to date. He began to work with Mayo.

"In Mayo I found my intellectual mother and in Henderson my intellectual father," Roethlisberger later wrote. "Whereas Mayo was more vigorous in his thinking, Henderson was more rigorous. From Mayo I got my insights and inspirations; from Henderson I received the invigoration that one gets from a dash of cold water."[66]

Roethlisberger would soon put insight, inspiration, and invigoration to use while serving as a key investigator in the Hawthorne project. No one did more than Roethlisberger to assemble the Hawthorne findings, discern their meaning, and disseminate the results in academia and the wider public. He synthesized what Henderson and Mayo created and applied their ideas to the phenomena through the modalities of listening, observing, and testing. In doing so, he made significant contributions to the evolution of American business, proved himself a consummate problem-solver, and helped to establish the Medical Model/the field of Human Relations.

The Medical Model: Listen, Observe, Test

What then is the Medical Model, which Henderson, Mayo, and Roethlisberger established? One of the key insights of this new process concerned dynamic equilibrium, the process by which systems comprising mutually interdependent variables adapt, integrate, and adjust to changes in their internal or external environments. Henderson saw organizations as systems that produced their own equilibria as they responded to changes in market demand, technology, investment conditions, and, crucially, the interests and character of their workforce. As such, a business could not be said to follow some ideal pattern of organization. A business was more like a living being, struggling through trial and error to achieve stability, profits and, especially in the early 20th century, labor peace. And exactly how it would achieve these goals was not preordained, because internal and external factors were always changing and affecting each other—the mutual interdependence at work. Because multiple processes were always unfolding at once, yesterday's stabilizing and profit-making business decision might not work today.

A complex business could no more afford to be static than could an organic system. If an organic system cannot adapt to changes of, say, temperature, achieving its safe equilibrium point by changing its internal or external conditions, it will suffer and potentially die. So too a complex organization must be dynamic, lest adverse circumstances accrue and sap its capacity to function. Today, we are accustomed to thinking in such terms, freely comparing organic and inorganic systems, but in Henderson's time, the thought was novel.

At the same time, Henderson and his colleagues understood that they could take the analogy only so far. While medical science can develop firm, generalizable knowledge of physiological systems, those of us studying organizations cannot afford to be so confident. The HBS pioneers were wise enough to recognize this. Whereas the physical and biological mechanisms of homeostasis are rigidly predictable, the variables that make up social systems are not so amenable to universal principles.

Instead of articulating encompassing theories, then, Henderson chose to make use of the "walking sticks" previously named. A walking stick is a conceptual framework for guiding practical problem-solving. The value of a walking stick lies in its utility, not in its explanatory power. The idea is to help the organization get from point A—a state of disequilibrium to be corrected—to point B, where equilibrium is achieved. Henderson's walking sticks arose from empirical observations. He didn't need to have an overarching theory of behavioral causes and effects; instead, he developed methods for studying a given circumstance and inferring what the sources of the problem needing correction were.

In a theory-driven context, the poor outcome tells one directly what the problem is. The manager or consultant can figure out the problem from balance sheets and organizational flowcharts alone, and from there the solution too will presumably be obvious. When someone uses Henderson's walking sticks, however, they must work harder. They must study the organization holistically in order to discern what human behaviors are causing the problem. Only then do they know what to correct and how to even begin trying.

The clinical approach, or medical method—deploying these walking sticks—demands that those of us who use this approach work backward from the presenting difficulty toward underlying causes. For example, where the problem is low productivity, we might find any number of causes and therefore solutions. If the source of the problem turns out to be interdepartmental conflict, we will prescribe some integrative mechanism, or improved methods of conflict resolution. If we encounter general managers who are overwhelmed by the demands of their jobs, we will go deeper still: Are these managers working on just their own tasks, or are other tasks falling to them because subordinates are insufficiently trained to handle their jobs? If managers are working only on their own tasks, what are the causes of inefficiency? Or are they receiving too many assignments? Alternatively, we may discover that the source of low productivity is an incentive pay system that is failing to motivate relevant employees in the manner intended. In that case, we would work with employees to diagnose where the system of expectations and rewards has gone awry, and test potential alternative pay structures.

Following the phenomena in the direction of solutions means applying inductive as opposed to deductive reasoning. Deductive reasoning is the stuff of theory. The investigator begins with some premise that he believes is true and applies that premise to the case in point. For instance, if your theory is that work is drudgery and workers are lazy, you prescribe anti-shirking mechanisms—a combination of positive incentives, such as increased wages for more productive workers, and discipline. This pretty well describes the methods of management science that helped to drive so much disquiet in America's factories. It is precisely because the deductive approach works so poorly that Henderson and others sought a new way, which came to be known as the medical method.

That new way was inductive. Inductive reasoning begins with observations of specific circumstances and draws more general principles on the basis of these observations. Inductive reasoning can be pursued through open-ended investigations that help build theories. It can also be pursued through experiments, as when a researcher artificially creates ideal conditions, applies some test, and documents the outcome in order to test a theory. This can be instructive, helping the researcher to isolate which variables matter in producing the outcome. But experiments must always bow to observations, for ultimately what matters are the empirical facts of the matter. Thus, experiments aim to prove hypotheses but may end up disproving them. As the great biologist and evolutionary thinker Thomas Huxley put it, the "tragedy of science" is "the slaying of a beautiful hypothesis by an ugly fact."[67]

The key acid test for the medical method was the Hawthorne Study, an extensive and long-running project lead by Mayo and Roethlisberger in the late 1920s and early 1930s. The study examined conditions at the Hawthorne Plant, outside Chicago, which manufactured telephone equipment for Western Electric Company, a subsidiary of AT&T. It was an inductive and iterative process involving dedicated researcher engagement, meticulous data collection, and a patient search for patterns. Overall, the study lasted some five years; it was no fly-by-night affair, and nothing was predetermined. We will be looking at this study in the next chapter.

CHAPTER 2

Listen

The Western Electric Company had made serious attempts to apply the principles of scientific management. Most importantly, it had pursued the holy grail of efficiency by consolidating all of its telephone manufacturing under the roof of a single plant, the Hawthorne Works, which was built in Cicero, Illinois, on the outskirts of Chicago, in 1905. By 1914, 12,000 workers were employed there, and by 1929, more than 40,000. The shift to single-factory manufacturing at such huge scale brought with it a fundamental reorganization, spearheaded by superintendent Henry F. Albright, a Taylor devotee. After 1923, semiskilled and unskilled workers replaced skilled machinists. Under the new regime, performance of repetitive tasks was scrupulously analyzed for time and motion efficiency by the company's growing band of industrial engineers and personnel managers.[1]

Like the Ford Factory workers who resisted the assembly line in 1916, Hawthorne employees were antagonistic to these changes. But Western Electric's executives professed both their understanding and their commitment to good relations between labor and management. One of the "commandments" established by the Western Electric General Personnel Committee was "to carry on the daily work in a spirit of friendliness"—albeit that many sources note the company's paternalism and anti-union bias.[2]

AT&T, Western Electric's parent company, was at least outwardly keen to head off labor unrest through the maintenance of employee satisfaction. In an address at the convention of the National Personnel Association in 1922, AT&T Vice President of Personnel E. K. Hall sounded remarkably like Mayo and Henderson, arguing that:

> The human factor is so inextricably tied in with all the processes of the entire works and is such a vital factor in the whole process of industry that it is simply impossible to take that factor and set it out to one side.[3]

Yet, according to Hall, industry had overemphasized mechanization and efficiency and neglected the human factor, thereby becoming "a house divided against itself." His solution was a new kind of professional, the personnel manager, whose task was to mobilize "the entire human element" on the basis of "the Golden Rule—doing to the other fellow just about as you would like to have the other fellow do to you if you were in his place."[4] That this sentiment arose from corporate self-interest shouldn't obviate the fact that it was also sincere. Evidence of this came in the form of inviting outsiders into Hawthorne to tell management and workers alike what was wrong and what might be done.

When Hawthorne plant superintendent Clarence J. Stoll heard that the National Research Council was leading a study of the effects of electric illumination on industrial productivity, he eagerly volunteered Hawthorne as a laboratory, even offering to cover the costs of light installation and the maintenance of production records. (Stoll's excitement may have been encouraged by the presence of Thomas Edison on the council's Committee on Industrial Lighting, which spearheaded the effort.)[5] In 1924, the Hawthorne Experiments commenced under the direction of Dugald C. Jackson, a professor of electrical engineering at MIT.

This was the sort of workplace where Mayo and Roethlisberger could try out their method recognizing and solving the problems of business. On the one hand, Hawthorne was beset with the enthusiasms of scientific management. On the other, managers on the ground—like Stoll—and upper management at AT&T were experimentalists. They were interested in trying new things if these might lead to a better-functioning business. Hawthorne turned out to be the ideal testbed for a kind of business consulting that focused on the phenomena.

At Hawthorne, Mayo and Roethlisberger patiently prototyped observational and listening methods until they had solid data on which to draw conclusions. They observed daily operations in the plant, carefully cataloging patterns of behavior. They ran experiments of their own, dividing up workers in order to isolate variables and figure out the interdependencies that governed the social system within the plant. And, with Mayo taking the lead, they developed a series of ever-improving survey and interviewing techniques, the better to elicit honest, useful information from employees. This—listening—was arguably the true obsession and genius of the HBS Hawthorne study.

Henderson took approving note of all this—a real laurel, given his congenitally acerbic character. Working with former colleagues from Harvard's medical school, he assisted in designing experimental methods and evaluating data. Those data helped make sense of some unexpected findings from the illumination study, which had failed to prove its hypotheses but had nonetheless provoked revelations. More spectacularly, the HBS team's findings led to new management policies that improved both worker satisfaction and productivity. It is no wonder that the business world—not just academics—took note.

Summing up the Hawthorne work in *Management and the Worker*, a surprise best-seller published in 1939, Roethlisberger noted the deeper meaning of what he, his colleagues, and Hawthorne's managers had learned. "Sometimes attempts to make ... employees more efficient unwittingly deprive them of those very things which give meaning and significance to their work," he wrote. "Their established routines of work, their cultural traditions of craftsmanship, their personal interrelations—all these are at the mercy of 'logical' innovations."[6] The modern corporation would do well to take such humane concerns seriously in its personnel practices and could do so by doing exactly what the Hawthorne researchers did: by orientating themselves "away from abstractions and toward concrete human situations."[7]

In Roethlisberger's view, Hawthorne was not just a study. It was a practical guide to management. The methods he and Mayo designed and implemented were not just methods of research; they were also methods of management. "Interview," Roethlisberger wrote,

> is a diagnostic and therapeutic tool which assists [the manager] in specifying and handling adequately particular human situations. It is a tool which is similar to that employed by the medical practitioner when he has to go from the symptoms to the realities behind them. It is a skill which assists him to analyze a complex human phenomenon into the elements that have produced it.[8]

Any manager could apply the medical model by listening, observing, and testing, thereby discerning both the workplace disease and the cure.

A Hive of Experimentation

Harvard's involvement with Hawthorne began at a November 1927 meeting of the Special Conference Committee, a group that had not adopted its obscure name by accident.[9] The men, who gathered at the Harvard Club in New York, occupied the heights of American business—CEOs and other executives of 10 of the largest corporations of the time, including General Motors, U.S. Steel, General Electric, the Rockefeller Oil Companies, and AT&T, the owner of the Hawthorne plant. The committee had been convened by the Rockefellers as part of their ongoing effort to address labor conflict. Meetings focused on industrial relations and coordination of labor policy and were kept secret so that members could explore these controversial subjects frankly, away from the scrutiny of the press and labor leaders.[10]

At least one outsider was present at this particular meeting: Elton Mayo. T. K. Stevenson, the personnel director at AT&T's Western Electric subsidiary, had taken an interest in Mayo's ideas about the psychological maladjustments of workers in response to industrial conditions. In particular, Stevenson sought Mayo's reaction to the experiments that Western Electric had carried out in the Relay Assembly Test Room at Hawthorne. These experiments sought to determine the effects of fatigue and rest periods on productive output, a matter well-suited to Mayo's and Henderson's interests.[11]

The relay-assembly experiments were themselves offshoots of the earlier illumination tests. Those tests had revealed no connection between lighting and productivity levels; productivity levels were rising at Hawthorne regardless of illumination levels. What the tests did reveal was just how hard it was to isolate the impact of a single variable like lighting.[12] One of the experimental reports concluded with the observation that "the effects of increased supervision and the psychological factors incident to test conditions are of much larger degree of magnitude than the increases which might possibly be ascribed to illumination."[13]

The National Research Council was only concerned with lighting, so they abandoned both the project and the discovery of the importance of supervision. But two managers at Hawthorne wanted to know more: Stoll, who had initiated the illumination studies, and engineer George

A. Pennock. Both were interested not just in "scientific" management but also science. They believed that, with controlled research, they could test factors affecting worker behavior and productivity. In particular, they believed that they could learn something about these factors by limiting observation to a small group in which "the number of variables which inevitably creep into a large group situation could be somewhat diminished."[14] Thus, on April 25, 1927, Stoll, Pennock, and other interested managers, began a new inquiry, conducted in the Relay Assembly Test Room.

At this point, Stoll and his group had not quite taken onboard the finding concerning the effects of supervision. Instead, they were still looking into more obvious features of working life that could be influencing productivity—specifically, the productivity of the five female workers who performed the repetitive and monotonous task of assembling telephone relays. Over the course of 12 test periods, the experimenters—all supervisors at the plant—altered the time, duration, or frequency of the workers' rest periods and recorded the associated productive output. An observer sat opposite the women's workbench and kept detailed notes. The experimenters also asked questions about workers' home lives and their required monthly visits to the company hospital, which were instituted in an effort to collect information about workers' physical condition. And the researchers posed other questions directly related to fatigue: "Do employees actually get tired out?" "Are rest pauses desirable?" "Is a shorter working day desirable?" "Why does production fall off in the afternoon?"[15]

Once again, the researchers were flummoxed by what they found. They had hoped to learn something about how to design rest periods for maximum productivity, but instead they discovered that there was no correlation between productivity and their manipulations of rest periods. Productivity increased steadily no matter what rest arrangement was tested. Pennock sent Mayo a report on the bewildering outcome in fall 1928, along with a note indicating that the project would be shut down because of inconclusive results.[16]

Mayo, having just returned from his inspiring sojourn in London, greeted Pennock's message with excitement.[17] Far from useless, these results were encouraging, for they potentially corroborated the illumination study's finding concerning effects of increased supervisor attention. Mayo and his team at HBS came up with five hypotheses as to what might explain the productivity gains seen at the plant during the past several years of research:

1. Improved material conditions (better lighting and equipment).
2. Rest periods and pauses providing relief from cumulative fatigue.
3. Rest periods and pauses providing relief from monotony.
4. The increased wage incentive in Period III (more on this in the following).
5. Social factors, specifically, the improved supervisor–employee relationship built over the course of the experiment.[18]

The first hypothesis was pro forma and was immediately discarded because of the findings of the illumination experiments. To explore hypotheses 2 and 3, the researchers assessed the output rates of individual relay-assembly workers alongside data that might indicate fatigue or monotony, including the day of the week (assuming fatigue builds as work hours accumulate) and measurements of blood pressure and vascular skin reaction. Again, no correlation was found. Lack of evidence linking rest periods to output ruled out explanations involving relief of fatigue and monotony.[19]

Hypothesis 4 referred to a test among what was called the "Second Relay Assembly Group." This additional group enjoyed a pay increase, while no changes were made to their break schedule. As in the rest of the experiment, researchers observed steadily increasing output over the course of the study period. But when wages were restored to their pre-test level, output remained high, suggesting that the wage incentive was not driving increased productivity.[20] Additionally, in another experiment designed to test the effect of the wage incentive, all test conditions from the previous experiment were duplicated *except for* the payment change, and output again remained high.[21]

Attention shifted to hypothesis 5. The only factor consistent across the various studies—of illumination, rest periods, and wages—was workers' increased engagement with supervisors in the testing room. In focusing on the changes intentionally introduced (rest periods, pay scales), the experimenters had overlooked the fundamental change inherent in the test room situation. As Roethlisberger noted, "the investigators had not been studying an ordinary shop situation but a socially contrived situation of their own making." [22] Mayo was emphatic. "The most significant change that the Western Electric Company introduced into its 'test room' bore only a casual relation to the experimental changes," he wrote—the significant changes being the illumination, rest, and pay conditions, and the experimental changes being increased productivity. "What the Company actually did for the group was to reconstruct entirely its whole industrial situation," he concluded.[23] That is, the *social* situation in the plant. Mayo contented that, as workers adjusted to the new environment of the test rooms, "there was a period during which the individual workers and the group had to readapt themselves to a new industrial milieu, a milieu in which their own self-determination and their social well-being ranked first and the work was incidental."[24]

What Mayo and the others had discovered became known as the Hawthorne effect—the tendency of study subjects to change their behavior by virtue of their awareness of being observed. Researchers in every area of the behavioral sciences have to reckon with the Hawthorne effect. As for the actual Hawthorne researchers, they wanted to know more about the supervisor–employee relationship, which seemed to have such positive influence. One might say that higher productivity was the new equilibrium managers hoped to achieve, but they would need more information in order to ensure that all of the interconnected variables were properly balanced, enabling the desired outcome. An expanded investigation of workers' thought processes would go a long way, if only the researchers asked the right questions.

Listening Closely

To this point, the HBS team had had a mostly advisory role in the Hawthorne research. But in the next phase, the Interviewing Program, they would be more hands-on. Roethlisberger described the Interviewing Program as "a search for what was determining the satisfactions of the workers and possibly affecting their production."[25] This would require a change of orientation. The former experimenters would have to become "clinicians, in which role they had to learn how to get the workers to talk about matters that were important to them."[26] The learning in question was provided by the HBS scholars.

From September 1928 through January 1929, five Hawthorne supervisors conducted interviews with 1,600 workers. Then the interviewing program was expanded through the establishment of an Industrial Research Division with a staff of 58 employees devoted fulltime to various research programs. Over the next year, the division would conduct more than 10,000 interviews and analyze over 80,000 employee comments.

At first, the interviewers tended to pose leading and narrow questions that made clear what answers the researchers wanted to hear or else just didn't give employees space to answer honestly. This, Roethlisberger wrote, "tended to put a person in a 'yes' or 'no' frame of mind. Instead of obtaining the employee's spontaneous and real convictions, it tended to arouse a reaction of antagonism or a stereotyped form of response."[27] Mayo, meanwhile, objected to the categorization of interview comments by subject (e.g., factory cleanliness, opinion of one's supervisor) rather than by the individual employee, which prevented researchers from grasping the total situation of a given worker. "Opinions are not detachable," Mayo explained. "What a worker thinks on a given subject is a symptom of what he is; his ideas cannot be torn out of their personal context and exhibited as significant."[28]

During visits to the Hawthorne plant, Mayo met with researchers and preached and demonstrated an alternative interviewing technique, based on his psychological training. This method, inspired primarily by the work of Pierre Janet, emphasized nondirective listening.[29] Mayo summarized this approach as follows:

1. Give your whole attention to the person interviewed and make it evident you are doing so.
2. Listen—don't talk.
3. Never argue, never give advice.
4. Listen to:
   a. What he wants to say.
   b. What he does not want to say.
   c. What he cannot say without help.

5. As you listen, plot out tentatively and for subsequent correction the pattern that is being set before you. To test this, occasionally summarize what has been said and present it for comment. Always do this with caution—that is, abbreviate and clarify but do not add or "twist."[30]

Mayo sent Roethlisberger, his protégé, to work on the Interviewing Program for the entire summer of 1930. Roethlisberger, who by this point was well-versed in Mayo's interviewing technique, proved an excellent surrogate, especially in his ability to translate Mayo's clinical ideas into language that the Hawthorne researchers could understand and act upon. In July 1929, the interviewing department officially shifted to Mayo's "indirect approach," with the goal of encouraging employees to talk extemporaneously and at length about any subject of interest to them. "As long as the employee talked spontaneously, the interviewer was to follow the employee's ideas, displaying a real interest in what the employee had to say," Roethlisberger wrote. "The interviewer was not to interrupt to try to change the topic to one he thought more important."[31]

This procedure, with its obvious debts to psychology and reflecting practices currently common to nearly all talk therapy, yielded a wealth of information about the situation of employees at the Hawthorne plant. Some of that information could be fruitfully analyzed in statistical terms, but much of it couldn't. Here are highlights from just a few of the personal histories the researchers collected, which reveal the obsessive thinking and mental disequilibrium that Mayo believed caused significant interference in workers' lives:

- Mr. Brown—whose 17-year-old daughter died of meningitis and whose wife, after giving birth to twins the following year, suffered a nervous breakdown—tells of the depression he experienced during this period and complains about his supervisor, who "treated me like a dog."
- Mr. White has "logicalizing" rationalizations for his pervasive sense of grievance: the personnel records are like a rap sheet, the company is like a jail, he's been demoted by enemies, policies are unfair, college men get too much preference,

the foreman is influenced by subordinates he's friends with, married women should not be allowed to work.

- Mrs. Black, described by her supervisor as a "chronic kicker" and a "problem case," confides to the interviewer that she can't stand the supervisor. After explaining that "things aren't so good at home"—her father died when she was six and a half, two of her younger brothers have since died, and her stepfather is a mean alcoholic who makes her mother cry— she tells the interviewer, "You know, I think the reason that I can't stand Mr. Jones is because every time I look at him he reminds me of my stepfather."[32]

Issues like these called for an entirely new approach to management— long overdue, in Mayo's opinion. Supervision "has frequently come to mean 'ordering people about,'" he wrote, a method he described as "exceedingly stupid."[33] At Hawthorne, Mayo helped develop a more intelligent method. Whereas previously the supervisor had been an enforcer of the rules of scientific management in order to maximize productive output, now he was more like a counselor or coach, drawing out the inner troubles of the worker and helping him or her adapt to the industrial environment.

Alongside stories of woe, the study elicited some heartening feedback that demonstrated the importance of the workplace social environment in drawing out the best from employees. The case of "Jennie," as she is known in the transcripts, is exemplary in this regard. Jennie's bosses once considered her a "problem case," but she blossomed in the team atmosphere of the Relay Assembly Test Room.[34] Why? The interviews established that her troubles at work were related to her homelife, marred by the death of her sister, followed soon after by that of her mother. With her father out of work, she was the breadwinner for him and her three brothers. The interviews paint a portrait of a fundamentally good-natured, sensitive, and able young woman with hobbies, interests, and dreams, but also one beset by loss and the weight of responsibility.

The day-to-day activities of the Relay Assembly Test Room, if not those of her previous assignment, were a balm for Jennie. "I've enjoyed the whole three years I've been there," she told researchers.

Everything is so nice, including even, well I don't who they are
supposed to be, they're really not our bosses... There really isn't
anybody that is our boss. You know, there's nobody that jumps on
our necks and we don't have a rate to make [A]nd then the idea
of all being in one gang is a pleasure. You know everybody works
together and there is nobody stalling.[35]

Of Mr. Chipman, one of the supervisors, she says, "he makes me
laugh," adding, "he is a swell boss, but we don't tell him so. We kid him
along and tell him he is terrible."[36] Once Jennie had a supportive and
enjoyable social life at work, many of her chronic worries dissipated and
she became a spirited team member committed to doing her job well.[37]

Investigators were interested in individual situations like Jennie's, but
primarily they were looking for "uniformities" in the data, which would
reveal systemic problems in need of correction. And the pattern researchers saw was that workers kept bringing up "social sentiments" in connection with their work experience.[38] In an effort "to catch the subtler and
more spontaneous aspects of the employees' social organization," a final
set of experiments zeroed in on relationships among workers in a shop
environment.[39]

On November 13, 1931, 14 male employees began working in the new
Bank Wiring Observation Room, where they assembled telephone bank
wires in the presence of a supervisor, also male. Also in the room were an
observer and an interviewer, Western Electric Supervisor William Dickinson,
who would later collaborate with Roethlisberger on *Management and the
Worker*. The observer—who in this case was not a supervisor but merely
a witness—was tasked with gathering performance data and recording
interactions and conversations he considered significant. He was to record
behaviors objectively and take down comments verbatim. Meanwhile, the
interviewer was to document the emotional and social situation as perceived by workers, in the narratives they constructed and the meanings they
attributed to events. Then observations could be compared with employees'
statements in interviews. Ultimately, the researchers hoped to learn more
about the function of informal relationships—what purposes they served,
how they affected performance, how they influenced and were influenced
by formal organization and to what effect.[40]

In analyzing the data, the researchers found within the formal organization unofficial networks that subverted their prior assumptions about employees' motives. Their most striking discovery was that Hawthorne's pay scheme, in which individuals' wages were determined by group output, did not work to incentivize behavior in the ways that management had assumed. Under such a system, it was predicted that each worker would be motivated to maximize group output in order to maximize individual reward, with faster workers pressing slower workers to speed up. Instead, the scheme actually served to restrict output to a level informally determined by the workers as a group, suggesting that social pressures trumped economic incentives. Specifically, workers talked among themselves about what constituted "a fair day's work."[41] They criticized fellow workers who exceeded the "bogey"—the output level expected by management—and told the interviewer about their fears that increasing the daily output would lead to a cut in hourly wages or an increase in the bogey, meaning that that they would end up no further ahead.[42] Turning out too much work made you a "rate-buster," while turning out too little meant you were a "chiseler." Telling anything to a supervisor constituted "squealing," and acting bossy made you "stuck up."[43]

It turned out that worker motivation was a socially constructed norm. Rather than a collection of individuals working to advance their economic interests, factory organization could be better understood as a social system. As Roethlisberger put it, "The men ... elaborated, spontaneously and quite unconsciously, an intricate social organization around their collective beliefs and sentiments."[44] This organization involved not just productivity norms but also cliques and hierarchies, a sense of internal unity that occasionally resulted in animosity toward those in the regular department outside the room,[45] and job trading. Many transcript passages involve "kidding" with a hostile edge; jokes targeting Poles, Catholics, sexual orientation, age, skill, speed, and size (one wireman is called "Runt" and another "Jumbo") operate as a form of social control within the group, with implications for an individual's output. One wireman is disliked because he keeps to himself; another is a slow worker who reads a lot of books and uses vocabulary like "voluptuous" and "diagnostician," but he has an appealing personality, so he's forgiven for the low output and 100-dollar words.[46] By all these means, the wiring room achieved its own equilibrium: a fair day's work.

Managers were profoundly affected by both the patterns in the data and the detailed portrayal of social life within the plant. All of it indicated that managers could not hope to succeed simply by ordering people about. They needed to understand the lives of workers, and not superficially. For many supervisors, the interviews provided an opportunity to see their own practices through the eyes of employees, to understand supervisory problems they had in common with others. This was training in empathy and open-mindedness.[47] As a direct result of the interviewing program, supervisors improved their listening skills, too, the better to learn from workers what problems they faced. "By encouraging the worker to talk freely and by refraining from hasty disapprobation, the supervisor was in a better position to 'spot' the locus of the interference and consequently to handle his employees more intelligently," Roethlisberger wrote.[48]

The Medical Model After Hawthorne

The Hawthorne study shut down in 1932, in the midst of the Depression. Perhaps more could have been learned had the study continued, yet there were findings enough—over 10,000 interviews (each over 10 pages long), piles of statistical output data, and thousands of pages of observers' notes—to confirm the human relations group's confidence in the medical model. The social and psychological phenomena they had observed defied existing theories about organizations and the people within them, demonstrating both that the medical model was a superior diagnostic tool and that the theories were bunk. As Roethlisberger explained, "In medicine the recognition of a syndrome precedes any explanation of its etiology. The skill of the clinician is his capacity to identify what is before him in the here and now."[49] The medical model could avoid the errors that arise when "we try to solve problems intellectually, abstractly, and analytically instead of trying to identify and recognize what is taking place in the here and now."[50]

Back at Harvard, human relations became a key part of the curriculum. Mayo, in particular, sought to nurture students' observational, listening, and communication skills. He even integrated clinical exposure. His Clinical Interviewing Seminar for second-year MBAs, first offered in 1936, saw business students visiting psychiatric wards in order to gain firsthand experience with the kind of observational and interviewing skills that Mayo saw as the basis of managerial skill. Mayo also started up a first-year course, "Human Problems of Administration," covering the intellectual background of human relations and focusing on central practices and findings of the Hawthorne studies. The sudden profusion of courses demonstrated the growing prestige of human relations at HBS and ensured that more students—future business practitioners themselves—were exposed to it.

Even faculty who had not been involved in Hawthorne proved enthusiastic promoters of the human relations method and message. In 1935, HBS Professor Philip Cabot began hosting a discussion group for business executives in which conversation often centered on the social contract between workers and management. Cabot agreed that "the most important problems which face business administrators today are not economic or technical but social."[51] For Cabot, the Hawthorne studies demonstrated the wisdom underlying Henderson's and Mayo's convictions. "Organizations are organisms like the human body which must be studied as a whole," Cabot wrote. "Studies of their parts are interesting, but they are useless without knowledge of the whole."[52]

Alongside courses and discussions with practitioners, the Hawthorne studies found an audience via Dickinson and Roethlisberger's book, *Management and the Worker*. Publication was slow-going—the book was not released until 1939—as Western Electric spent three years reviewing the manuscript, and the wealth of data took time. "This sweating through a body of data was what I needed," Roethlisberger recalled. "For the first time I realized what research—not in the library—was about.... I have come to believe that for seekers of knowledge there is no substitute."[53]

Management and the Worker was, on its surface, a very detailed report of Hawthorne's experimental design and findings. But it also captured the essence of the group's approach to social research. The text is rife with references to nondirective interviewing, sentiments, social systems, and equilibrium. Employing the conceptual scheme developed by Henderson, the book meticulously sorts through detailed observation and interview transcriptions, allowing the reader to see the facts "as they are" as well as their interpretation by the researchers. The process of knowledge-development in the book—moving from observation to uniformities to conceptual scheme—mirrors the inductive approach of the research itself. And the authors, Roethlisberger and Western Electric's Dickinson, detail the evolution of field methods employed during the studies, laying out various stages of interview techniques and insights gained through practice.

"Although a narrative account of what was done step by step would bear the stamp of human imperfection," Roethlisberger wrote, "nevertheless it would describe what actually took place. It would picture the trials and tribulations of a research investigator at his work, and thus allow future investigators to see and to profit from the mistakes which were made."[54] By documenting not only the findings but also the process by which researchers arrived at them, Roethlisberger hoped to avoid the problematic tendency in the social sciences to prize the theory (the product) over discovery (the process): "The deductive way that a theory looks when completed . . . is not the way this theory is arrived at."[55]

Furthermore, by showing which research methods worked and which didn't, Roethlisberger and Dickson were providing practical guidance to managers. For, again, the Hawthorne studies not only produced knowledge about social organizations, they also enacted a management paradigm—one in which supervisors took seriously the minds of their workers and the social life of the plant.

The human relations perspective seemed to strike a chord with managers, gaining popularity in practitioner circles throughout the 1940s and 1950s. HBS closed during World War II, but the decade following the school's reopening proved to be the heyday of human relations, both within HBS and elsewhere. By the early 1950s, dozens of colleges and universities had established research centers for industrial relations, versions of the human relations group at Harvard. Notable centers included Kurt Lewin's Center for Group Dynamics at the University of Michigan, William Whyte's Human Relations Group at Cornell, and Doug McGregor's Industrial Relations Center at MIT. The methodologies and theoretical orientations of these groups differed in some ways. Still, they were characterized by a "striking ideological consistency"—a common philosophy of scientific discovery, a shared interest in the worker and in groups of workers, and a collective goal of leveraging the behavioral sciences to advance both knowledge and practice in the industrial setting.[56]

Management and the Worker continued to grow in popularity, too, bringing the story of the Hawthorne experiments to business communities around the globe. In the years after the war, "productivity teams" from all over the world came to American business schools to learn the tricks of the trade—the secrets to the industrial productivity that had brought the United States such spectacular success during wartime. Much to Roethlisberger's delight, these teams were most interested in learning about the Hawthorne experiments, and they often asked for an audience with him instead of "the big chieftains" in marketing, finance, or accounting and control.[57]

The period after the war saw both the consolidation of the human relations paradigm and the medical model and their extension into new arenas. On the consolidation side, in 1948 Roethlisberger began teaching the MBA elective "Human Relations." The course used cases, many from Western Electric, to teach "personal, empirical, and intuitive" skills that enabled cooperation and understanding in interpersonal interactions and sought to develop in students a "clinical point of view."[58] It was, in other words, a class about "skilled listening."[59] Students must have found this perspective both interesting and useful because there was always a long waitlist for the course, which was soon expanded to include a second term.

In 1951, Roethlisberger developed a new training program in human relations that would prove influential. The "Human Relations Clinic," as it came to be called, offered doctoral students an opportunity to apply their specialized knowledge in practical settings. Students could choose from one of five "learning contexts": research, counseling, membership, leadership, and personal life. Regardless of the context, students were trained first in the skillful observation of phenomena and second in how to act upon or interpret those phenomena (i.e., the clinical method). The program was small and only lasted three years, but its methodologies and graduates would ripple out across practice and scholarship for decades.

As for extension to new arenas, this was accomplished by both Roethlisberger and other successors to Mayo who had taken up the mantle of human relations. One of these number was George Homans, who had been a student of Mayo's. In *The Human Group* (1950), Homans applied the methods of the medical model to develop a conceptual scheme of small groups through the careful analysis of five concrete case studies. Although Homans never bought Henderson's sociological ideas wholesale, he did adopt the notion of theory as walking stick and believed that "no theory is likely to endure which does not arise directly out of long-continued, intuitive familiarity with the welter of facts which it attempts to order."[60] Homans moved inductively from careful observation of concrete phenomena, to identifying uniformities in the data, to making tentative propositions about the properties of groups and the relationships between those properties.

Homans' conclusions in *The Human Group* became the inspiration for a later collaboration with Roethlisberger, one that took human relations deep into new territory. Homans' idea was to use the techniques of the medical model to test three propositions about group behavior: the theory of distributive justice, the theory of social certitude, and the theory of external and internal rewards, all of which make predictions about worker behaviors and sentiments within groups. The distributive justice theory holds that when the investment of one group member is greater than that of his peers, but his return from group membership is less than that of his peers, that member will feel the imbalance as injustice and either reduce his involvement or find a way to enhance his return. On the other hand, when the investment of a member is less than his peers but the return greater, that member will feel the imbalance as guilt and try to reduce that guilt by investing more or accepting less in return. For its part, the theory of social certitude hypothesizes that group members want clear and unambiguous relations with each other—that is, to know where they stand in relation to others—in order to minimize anxiety. Finally, the theory of external and internal rewards proposes that both kinds of incentive are motivating: external rewards (money, job status, and interesting work) and, significantly, internal rewards (the need to feel that one belongs, to be liked, to be an accepted member of the group) accompany higher productivity and job satisfaction.

Whereas the medical model had found the theories of scientific management utterly lacking, the researchers in this case found that these theories had a degree of merit, although there were also glitches. For instance, the theory of distributive justice turns out to be highly elastic, as different individuals have different dispositions toward justice. Some shrug off others' shirking with equanimity; others feel acutely wronged. Some suffer guilt for their lack of contributions; others will try to ride the gravy train as long as possible. In reading through the "soft, gooey" data—interview transcripts and observations—Roethlisberger concluded that these individual differences are determined by personal history and psychology.[61] The theory's predictions were indeed sound, but only after adjusting for these personal factors.

The research was published in the 1958 book, *The Motivation, Satisfaction, and Productivity of Workers*. The chief finding dovetailed with that of the Hawthorne studies, despite the differences in research design. Investigators concluded that:

> [Group] output was determined far more by the production norms of the group than by the production standards of management, whose needs were satisfied far more by the social structure of the group than by the rewards which management offered and whose regular members and leaders exercised their influence and leadership ... by trying to preserve the group's social life.[62]

Research like this confirmed the flexibility and power of the medical model. Even those less open-minded than Henderson and Mayo—that is, those who approached social contexts with relatively firm theories in mind—could use the model to test their ideas. And, importantly, the theories that Homans, Roethlisberger, and the others explored were far better attuned to social dynamics than earlier theories such as scientific management had been. With the help of Mayo and Roethlisberger, Henderson's medical–sociological perspective on business had sunk in. Not only had it become possible to think about organizations as social systems, but, for a growing number of researchers and practitioners, it was impossible not to. Listening, observing, and testing had proven that businesses had complex human dynamics, products of individual minds and relationships within and across groups and hierarchies.

CHAPTER 3

Observe

During the Second World War, HBS shut down its regular MBA teaching programs and instead turned to training new officers in the U.S. Army and Navy in six "wartime schools," as they were called. From 1943 to 1946, the regular MBA program was canceled and all remaining faculty including Henderson, Mayo, Roethlisberger, and their associates focused on the war effort. Already in 1942 though, it was clear that as part of this effort there would be an increased need for new case studies, which could be used in teaching courses that would come under the purview of the department of *Industrial Management and Administration*, the forerunner of the organizational behavior department. One of these was the Dashman case developed by George Lombard. It is this case with which we will begin this chapter. After that, in both this chapter and the next, I will highlight some "greatest hits" of human relations research, demonstrating the breadth of situations in which the medical model can bring problems to light, diagnose their sources, and recommend remedies. Throughout this chapter, we'll explore insights about worker satisfaction (hint, it turns out workers don't all respond to the same rewards) and about conflict resolution in large, innovative organizations struggling to achieve internal cohesion (hint, it turns out what and how you observe matters profoundly when you are searching for a solution). What this and the next chapter, as well as the examples chosen, underscore is the role the medical model continued to play in the development of our field and more generally its usefulness both in understanding how companies work and in developing solutions to the problems that beset them.

Dashman: The Challenge of Management Transitions

Taught now for decades, the Dashman case underscores the importance of the medical model in helping managers understand challenges that arise during management transitions, something that was important during the Second World War and has gone one to become a key theme of later human relations work. The case was written by a young George Lombard, who was originally hired at HBS in the 1930s as an associate dean of students but later went on to become the Louis E. Kirstein professor of human relations. He was self-evidently a good listener and interviewer, and he worked closely with Roethlisburger while helping HBS students find job placements. Impressed, Roethlisberger convinced both Lombard and the school that Lombard's skills would be better put to use helping to develop the field of human relations, and he eventually was sent out into the field as an observer. One of Lombard's first assignments was observing the workers in the Macy's little girls' dress department, where he felt he made a success of his task because no one expected a young man to know about girls' dresses.[1] As a result, he was left in peace to observe the department's employees at work and develop an understanding of the dynamics that were causing issues in the department. What Lombard did by inclination—observe closely and unobtrusively—generations of business school graduates and scholars would be introduced to by way of the Dashman case. At its core, the case conveys that the opposite of being given the gift of an opportunity to observe in peace is failing to observe at all.

In the 1940s, the Dashman Company was manufacturing a large array of equipment and material for the United States' armed forces. It had 20 plants dispersed throughout the central United States. Previously, each plant manager had been encouraged by the head office to operate independently in most matters, and specifically with purchasing procedures. By late 1940, however, it was becoming clear that the company would confront rising difficulties in procuring essential raw materials needed by the plants. To implement greater coordination, the company's president, Mr. Manson, appointed Mr. Post, an experienced purchasing executive, as vice president in charge of purchasing.

Such was Mr. Manson's faith in Mr. Post that not only was this position specifically created for him, but Mr. Post was left alone to organize his job and manage his new responsibilities. To help execute them, however, Mr. Post was also assigned Mr. Larson, who not only had worked at Dashman for years but personally knew most of the plant managers.

The hiring of Mr. Post, and the company's intentions to coordinate purchasing going forward, was telegraphed throughout Dashman, including a notice of these facts in the company's internal publication.

Mr. Post immediately began to centralize Dashman's purchasing procedure. Drawing upon the experience for which Mr. Mason had hired him, Mr. Post decided "he would require each of the executives who handled purchasing in the individual plants to clear with the head office all purchase contracts which they made in excess of $10,000."[2] Additionally, to ensure the head office could effectively coordinate across the 20 plants, Mr. Post informed each plant manager that he must notify Mr. Post's office about contracts being prepared at least a week before they were to be signed. These steps would help ensure that coordination across plants, and with the head office, would be mutually beneficial to all. Mr. Post presented his proposal to Mr. Mason, who in turn presented it to the board of directors, and there was common agreement. The plan was approved just three weeks prior to Dashman's peak buying season.

With promptness, Mr. Post drafted, and asked Mr. Larson to review and approve, a letter to be sent to every purchasing agent at all 20 of Dashman's plants. The letter Mr. Larson reviewed read as follows:

Dear _____:

The board of directors of our company has recently authorized a change in our purchasing procedures. Hereafter each of the purchasing executives in the several plants of the company will notify the vice president in charge of purchasing of all contracts in excess of $10,000 which they are negotiating at least a week in advance of the date on which they are to be signed.

I am sure that you will understand that this step is necessary to coordinate the purchasing requirements of the company in these times when we are facing increasing difficulty in securing essential supplies. This procedure should give us in the central office the information we need to see that each plant secures the optimum supply of materials. In this way the interests of each plant and of the company as a whole will best be served.

Yours very truly ...[3]

Mr. Lawson raised no objection to the contents of the letter. He did suggest, however, that Mr. Post, who had met only a handful of the company's purchasing agents, visit all of them. In effect, Mr. Lawson suggested Mr. Post hand deliver the letter or give each plant's relevant staff the opportunity to discuss the new arrangement with Mr. Post personally. Citing all that he had to do around the home office, Mr. Post dismissed the suggestion. There was no time for such a trip. The letter was sent out forthwith.

Throughout the 20 plants, Mr. Post's letter was received and, judging by the written responses from plant managers and purchasers, approved of. Mr. Post's suggestions were deemed practical. The home office's interest in a week's notice of any intention to sign a contract was acknowledged. Each plant, in turn, assured Mr. Post of their intention to cooperate. And then, nothing happened. For six weeks, no notice of any contracts being negotiated was submitted to the head office. Following trips to the different plants, other Dashman executives returned to report that everything remained busy, and the old routines were being followed.

Students reading and working with this case are asked to consider, what, if anything, should Mr. Post, and the CEO of Dashman, do? Their reactions are always in one of two camps. They either suggest that the subordinate managers meet with Mr. Post, and with each other, to discuss the impact of his actions. Or, after noting that the case itself suggested that there was no interest in this idea among the subordinate managers, the remaining students suggest that Mr. Post's alternative was to just wait and let the situation play out. Prominent in the case, and most easily identifiable to students, is what Mr. Post did. Faced with a deadline—he was hired to centralize purchasing and needed to alert managers of the new, and what his experience told him were reasonable, procedures—he acted promptly ahead of peak purchasing. Hidden in the case description, however, is the not-simple, but nontrivial, recommendation of Mr. Lawson: Mr. Post, before he sends out the new procedures that the head office expects of each plant, should meet personally with each plant's purchasing agent. And too easily overlooked is a central insight in Mr. Lawson's recommendation. Such a trip, however inconvenient, would allow, even force, Mr. Post to observe individuals reaching decisions in context.

The failure of Mr. Post's initiative enables instructor and students to explore the nature of the evolving situation and its impact on the company, and ultimately its effect on Mr. Post. In the process, the students are always forced to think about relationships in large complex organizations and asked to consider ways in which Mr. Post's problems could have been avoided. The case is designed to lead the students to the realization that listening carefully and observing closely are important walking sticks for managers. Mr. Post's failure to listen closely to the recommendations of his subordinate, who, as a longtime employee of the company, understood its unspoken rules, is a direct cause of the failure of his initiative. That Mr. Lawson also recommends using the trips to observe how decisions are reached at the individual plants is a clear nod to the importance of observation as well. The students realize these facts only when they work closely with the case themselves and thus, they learn how important the ability to listen and observe carefully can be to a manager in the real world, they will shortly be entering.

Understanding Job Satisfaction

The Dashman case is just one example of how the second generation of human relations scholars went about ensuring their fields' relevance to the students who would soon become practitioners in real life. Two other disciples of human relations who picked up where Henderson, Mayo, and Roethlisberger left off were Paul Lawrence—my mentor—and Art Turner. In 1965, they published *Industrial Jobs and the Workers* a book whose rather plain title belied the exciting findings within its pages. Lawrence and Turner were interested in the question of job satisfaction. The very notion of job satisfaction had little relevance in the old world of scientific management, in which the only satisfaction that mattered to supervisors was that derived from getting the most out of the worker at the lowest possible pay rate. By the 1960s, the more holistic attitude of human relations had seeped into the wider working culture, yet still, very little was known about the sources of job satisfaction.

Lawrence and Turner postulated that the most intellectually demanding jobs provided the greatest satisfaction. This was a reasonable working hypothesis—a walking stick, in Henderson's language—reflecting decades of humanistic thinking about labor. After all, scientific managers had proven disastrously wrong in their assumption that workers always wished to do as little as possible; in fact, many assembly workers found the monotony intolerable and yearned to instead exercise their skills. To evaluate their hypothesis, Lawrence and Turner launched a study that examined 47 different jobs in 11 industries, identifying job attributes such as task variety, worker autonomy, interactions (required and optional), required knowledge, required skills, and responsibility level. The high degree of positive covariance among these attributes allowed them to be combined into an index of task complexity, which the researchers titled requisite task attributes (RTAs).

The major hypothesis, that workers would respond favorably to high-RTA jobs, was confirmed in one sense: attendance. Workers showed up more often when the job was relatively complex and demanding. However, Lawrence and Turner did not find the expected linear relationship between RTA scores and reported job satisfaction. Workers with high-RTA jobs did report relatively high job satisfaction, but so did those with low-RTA jobs. The most dissatisfied were those in the middle of the curve. This puzzle led to further investigation, which revealed what Lawrence and Turner called "subcultural predispositions": they found that workers' communities of origin influenced what they expected from a job.[4]

This turn in their discovery highlights the importance of close observation of all areas of a worker's life. If Lawrence and Turner had asked only yes and no questions directly related to a worker's level of satisfaction with his or her work, they would almost certainly not have discovered the influence a worker's community background had on their general job satisfaction. This information was only gleaned by paying close attention to workers in context and yielded unique and actionable insights. What their observations, which, it should be remembered, were conducted in the 1950s and 1960s, showed was that workers who came from communities with strong Catholic traditions generally viewed work as a means to economic ends, whereas employees from mainly Protestant communities tended to see work as a source of intrinsic satisfaction. While in today's world it is far less likely researchers would observe the same communities acting as touchstones for worker satisfaction, the more general observation remains applicable. Demographic variance among workers was the most significant insight, providing compelling evidence that the rewards of work are in the eyes of workers themselves. If one wants to motivate employees effectively, one must provide rewards that they value. And to identify what these rewards are, one needs to observe workers as Mayo, Lombard, Lawrence, and Turner did: carefully, patiently, and in context.

Research, Development, and Contingency

In the fall of 1958, I started my own education at HBS. By the Fall of 1959, a year later, I had gained a basic understanding of how the Organizational Behavior faculty at HBS conceived of their field and had grown interested in pursuing my own research in the field. By this time Roethlisburger was the only one of the pioneers still involved, and the Organizational Behavior faculty consisted of over 20 scholars, most educated at HBS, but a few from other universities in the United States.

The immediate question for me was who would be willing and able to supervise my thesis research. The obvious answer was Roethlisburger. But after one meeting with him, it was clear that his dance card was full. I asked him to offer suggestions and he encouraged me to meet with George Lombard and Paul Lawrence. At the time, Lombard was teaching the Organizational Behavior Unit's largest elective course. It was offered in the second year of the MBA program and its topic was "listening." Built on Mayo's ideas, it introduced and sought to improve students' skill at understanding others by listening to them. Roethlisburger suggested I meet with Lombard, which I did. It was clear to me, however, that Lombard was not the right thesis chair for me. He was a great listener, but I wanted more active help in thinking more deeply about possible dissertation topics. As it happened, Paul Lawrence was conducting research at a manufacturer of laboratory equipment, collecting boxes of data about employees' efforts to coordinate their activities and the problems they encountered along the way. Lawrence suggested I look at these data and see what patterns I could find. This was the impetus that I needed, and I was off and running on my dissertation research.

What I discovered was a persistent concern among managers about the conflicts between various functional units of the business—sales, engineering, and manufacturing. It seemed they constantly disagreed and rarely managed to resolve their differences. This was something of a eureka moment: intergroup discord was an important business challenge on which little research had been conducted. To begin with, I wrote a couple of case studies about dysfunctional conflicts between departments and how to resolve them, challenging students to think about structural solutions and relationship. But there was a lot more to learn.

I decided to apply my interest in conflict resolution and functional integration to larger organizations, which, at this point, were not generally understood as importantly distinct from smaller businesses. Somebody needed to come up with a new way of conceptualizing the structural issues of large organizations, which were becoming increasingly important in the economy. This interested me at once, not least because I had served in the U.S. army in the early 1950s and so had experienced what it was like to be a cog in an extremely big and complex machine. I was inspired in part by an observation from Herbert Spencer, the influential 19th-century English social thinker, who seemed to understand better than most that integration and differentiation each mount as organizations grow.

> A social organism is like an individual organism in these essential traits: that it grows; that while growing it becomes more complex; that while becoming more complex, its parts acquire increasing mutual dependence; that its life is immense in length compared with the lives of its component units; that in both cases there is increasing integration accompanied by increased heterogeneity.[5]

As a convinced Hendersonian, hence at home with the idea of a social system as a living organism, I found these words true to life.[6]

My focus for my doctoral work then was functional integration in innovative companies. Firms involved in product and process innovation face especially complex organizational problems because the goals of research and development (R&D) are so vastly different from those of other functional departments. It is hard enough for R&D teams to talk with each other, much less with sales, marketing, and other functional units committed to the success of earlier generations of products.

I studied several major chemical companies involved in developing, manufacturing, and marketing plastic polymers, including American Cyanimide, Dow Chemical, Rohm and Haas, and Union Carbide. Each company needed tight coordination among functional units if they were to secure business success. My hypothesis was that the firm with organizational structures accommodating both differentiation—specialized goals—and integration among units would achieve the best results. I developed a questionnaire to assess the goals and timetables of the major functional units in these companies, using the same measurements for each company to ensure that my datasets were comparable. I used interviews to measure the interpersonal styles of the managers in the various functional units of the companies. And I created another questionnaire to measure each manager's perception of the degree of integration between their unit and the other functional units in the business.

Cumulatively, the questionnaires and my interviews at each of the companies were an effort to apply a rigorous model of observation that would produce actionable data. The questionnaires alone would not have provided as many details and as much insight into the internal workings of the companies involved as the combination of the two processes did; for an in-depth examination, I needed the interviews as well. Conversely, the questionnaires were equally necessary. As organizations grew more complex, the manner and means of observing them became commensurately more complex. Lombard observing dress purchases at Macy's was becoming the organizational behaviorist gathering observational data for subsequent review.

Visible within the data was the fact that at these companies, managers attempted to smooth over differences across divisions by creating integrative units, units whose express purposes were to foster collaboration. In an article Lawrence and I wrote for *Harvard Business Review* in 1967, we summarized the importance of "the integrative function" as being "on a par with such traditional functions as production, sales, research, and others."[7] The importance of integration in ever more complex and rapidly changing organizations was apparent; the best way to achieve integration, however, was more an exercise of skilled observation. Inevitably, these integrative units incorporated elements of the divisions whose collaboration they facilitated. I found that the effectiveness of an integrative unit was related to its intermediate position between the basic units it was designed to link. If the integrative unit was more similar to one of the basic units, it had to be less similar to other basic units, thus impairing its ability to unify efforts across boundaries among them. A delicate but deliberate balance of differentiation and integration needed to be struck, if effective integrators were to help organizations succeed. In a sense I was articulating the obvious, something hidden in plain sight. The optimal integrative unit between or among departments needed to sustain sufficient distance from each so that its workers could observe opportunities for integration, and act on behalf of the company's interests over any individual department's interest. Yet often, the obvious is not apparent to those occupying the organizational heights. Critics of the Hawthorne findings considered those to be obvious as well, but company higher-ups found them revelatory.[8] Typically, and perhaps wisely, decision makers do not act until they see evidence in front of them, even if it is evidence of the obvious.

Another variable I studied, the norms of conflict resolution, was related to integration in the system. Lawrence and I found that the growing complexity within organizations had rendered ever more ineffective older practices, such as the "shared boss" or a single general manager. The companies we studied had all developed separate units to facilitate cooperation among a company's basic functions. As we reported, "The emergence of these integrating jobs in considerable numbers now makes it practical to turn the spotlight of systematic research on them."[9] When we did, we discovered that the best-performing company had the most effective integration units. These were identifiable by executives whose orientations and time horizons allowed them to understand the basic functions and work being done across departments and who were thus consequently better at confronting and resolving conflicts among those departments.

Once I joined the faculty at HBS, my first project expanded on my earlier doctoral work to six plastics companies, including those already mentioned. Plastics entailed sophisticated and rapidly changing technology in a competitive marketplace, factors Mayo and Henderson might have described as disequilibrating. Plastics companies therefore had high need of internal balancing resources—in particular, means of conflict resolutions. Working with Jim Garrison, then a graduate student, I learned that problem-solving, more so than problem-avoidance, was successful in promoting integration among differentiated units. Smoothing over conflict was less effective than confrontation, as were management efforts to force resolutions.

Eventually, this and other research became the basis of *Organization and Environment*, the 1967 book I coauthored with Lawrence. In this book, we explored how the basic dynamics of differentiation, integration, and conflict resolution might vary in environments that placed different demands on organizations, using paired companies (high and low performers) in three disparate industries. We compared the plastics manufacturers we had already investigated to companies in two other industries: breakfast cereal and beer cans and bottles. The cereal industry was competitive but seldom innovative, while companies making containers for beer and similar products faced a low-competition environment and made a product that had barely changed in years, if not centuries. Lawrence and I even joked that there had been little evolution in production methods since the time of the ancient Egyptians. The beer-container companies thus exemplified firms operating in stable business environments—firms that could expect to keep going as they had for decades, with little growth or change. Plastics companies, by comparison, grew quickly and changed processes frequently to match shifting demand. Cereal companies lay somewhere in between, growing and developing new products, but at a rate much lower than that of the successful plastics companies.

Through a combination of interviews and questionnaires, my research partners and I collected data about differentiation and integration in the high- and low-performing organizations in each of the three industries, summarized in the following table (Table 3.1).[10]

As we predicted, the plastics companies had the greatest differentiation—an outcome of working across many product lines—the food organizations fell in the middle range, and the container organizations were the least differentiated. The high-performing organizations in each of the industries achieved similar levels of integration, and the low-performing organizations followed suit, achieving comparable integration and less than their more successful counterparts.

Table IV–6

AVERAGE DIFFERENTIATION AND INTEGRATION
ACROSS THREE ENVIRONMENTS *

Industry	Organization	Average differentiation	Average integration
Plastics	High performer	10.7	5.6
	Low performer	9.0	5.1
Foods	High performer	8.0	5.3·
	Low performer	6.5	5.0
Containers	High performer	5.7	5.7
	Low performer	5.7	4.8

* Comparable pairs of units are used in all six organizations (sales-produc-
tion, production–research, and sales–research). The average scores reported
here for plastics organizations are thus slightly different from those reported
in Chapters II and III, since fundamental research and integrative units
have been excluded to achieve comparability. Higher differentiation scores
mean greater differences. Higher integration scores mean better integration.

• To simplify this part of our discussion we have selected one of the
high-performing plastics organizations (A) and one of the low-performing
plastics organizations (A) to compare with the food and container organizations. These two organizations in most characteristics represented the extreme
organizational conditions found in the plastics industry.

*Table 3.1 The above Table IV-6 shows our comparison of
differentiation and Integration across three industries*

The organizations in plastics and food, with their relatively high
level of differentiation, had developed several integrative devices, while
the less-differentiated container organizations relied on simple information systems and the managerial hierarchy to achieve what integration
they needed—or were able to achieve.[11] When we examined how cross-
functional conflicts were resolved, we found that in both the plastics and
food organizations the middle levels of management took an active role; in
the container organizations, such conflicts were less frequent, and higher
management got involved. Thus, in the organizations with the greatest
potential for conflict (high differentiation, tight integration), managers
closest to the action resolved conflicts (Table 3.2). In the effective organizations, we also found a reliance on direct confrontation between the
parties to settle disputes.

What we took from this research was not that all organizations
need tight integration or even that organizations benefiting from tight

integration should follow the model of any of our particular high performers. Rather, we were sensitive to the point that different industries
have different needs when it comes to integration and conflict resolution.
In the low-differentiation container industry, a business did not need to
work so hard to address problems arising from the interaction of departments; to follow the methods of the high-performing chemical company
would involve greater expense than the container company needed to
concern itself with.

Table VI-1
COMPARISON OF INTEGRATIVE DEVICES IN
THREE HIGH-PERFORMING ORGANIZATIONS

	Plastics	*Food*	*Container*
Degree of differentiation *	10.7	8.0	5.7
Major integrative devices	(1) Integrative department	(1) Individual integrators	(1) Direct managerial contact
	(2) Permanent cross-functional teams at three levels of management	(2) Temporary cross-functional teams	(2) Managerial hierarchy
	(3) Direct managerial contact	(3) Direct managerial contact	(3) Paper system
	(4) Managerial hierarchy	(4) Managerial hierarchy	
	(5) Paper system	(5) Paper system	

* High score means greater actual differentiation.

Table 3.2 The above Table VI-1 reflects our comparison of integrative devices across the three industries

What we had come upon was, in fact, a new way of thinking about
large organizations—a contingency theory. Contingency theory took
issue with "the one best way" of classical business theorists, who in
their dependence on abstract generalizations echoed Frederick Taylor's
scientific management. Instead, we observed what worked in given organizations and thought hard about why it worked for that organization.

We recognized that some general principles might emerge; for instance, we realized that, in every environment we studied, conflict resolution was most successful when carried out at the lowest level of organization. But we found many successful approaches to cross-department integration hierarchy. On the whole, we concluded that managers, in designing and planning organizations, should not be concerned with following one specific method but rather should create mechanisms for functional integration appropriate to the precise tasks they are trying to perform.[12]

Looking back on contingency theory 50 years later, I believe Lawrence and I were developing the kind of framework, which Henderson, Mayo, and Roethlisberger would have approved—a walking stick derived from observing and diagnosing real organizations. Our methods were very much like Henderson's and Mayo's: we took a history, as it were, collecting data through interviews and questionnaires; we did our version of a physical exam, intently observing the processes and the structures of the organizations we studied and cataloging the behaviors within them. Without these methods, we would never have arrived at our understanding of the variety of challenges facing different organizations based on their individual needs, structures, and functions.

Contingency theory is also flexible, embracing the variables, internal and external, that arise in any organization. Others picked up on our ideas. Lawrence Fouraker, the sixth Dean of HBS, working with his colleague John Stopford examined the organizational forms of multinational companies, research that Stopford continued in collaboration with L. T. Wells. Later scholars, such as Lex Donaldson, Fred Fiedler, and J. Pfeffer developed the theory further, each focusing on diverse organizational characteristics such as leadership, human resource management, and strategic decision-making practices.[13] While research in contingency theory has been diverse in design and method—some of the work has been experimental, some based on field studies—it repeatedly demonstrates that organizational characteristics are contingent on an organization's purpose. The key to understanding how organizations work and how they can work better lies in understanding what is particular to the organization in question. And among the most valuable skills a manager or scholar of management possesses is careful, professional observation.

CHAPTER 4

Test

In the previous chapter, I discussed some of the revelatory work arising from the medical model in the generation that succeeded the founders of human relations. Those of us who arrived in the discipline in the 1940s, 1950s, and 1960s were lucky in many ways. We were able to learn directly from some of the founders, in particular Roethlisberger. And we had the good fortune to train younger colleagues eager to learn our approaches. Yet, as I'll describe in Chapter 5, at the moment the medical model was reaching its most productive phase, there arose a concerted and, alas, successful effort to discredit and replace it with the supposedly greater rigor of quantitative methods borrowed from academic economics and sociology. HBS, however, remained a relative bastion of the medical model. And researchers at HBS have proven time and again that the program of listening, observing, testing, and then diagnosing works well in real-world practical circumstances.

What follows in this chapter is both a close look at the development of human relations in the second half of the 20th century and into the 21st and a summary of some pathbreaking work by my own successors. We will examine the research of first Dick Walton and then John Kotter, who influentially used the medical model to better understand the behaviors of successful managers and to clarify the relationship between management and leadership. I'll take a turn describing some of my own insights from investigations of white-collar environments such as law firms and investment banks. Then we will consider later human relations work by Jack Gabbaro and Linda Hill, whose research elucidates the experience of becoming a manager and highlights the interpersonal and observational skills—as well as the emotional resources—that make for successful management transitions. And the medical model will prove its value at a contemporary software company with a globally distributed workforce.

Designing a New Work Culture

In the mid 1960s, my colleague Dick Walton, then at Purdue University, was hired by General Foods as a consultant at their pet-food plant in Kankakee, Illinois.[1] Management was having trouble overcoming divisions between functional departments at the plant—divisions that made it hard for different departments to work with and learn from each other. But during a visit to the plant, Walton noticed symptoms of other problems, too. "I saw pet food on the floor, scribbling across the wall and so on," Walton remembers.[2]

Drawing on his observations at the factory, Walton diagnosed severe worker alienation manifested by "employee indifference and inattention while manning the continuous-process technology."[3] As he learned more, he realized that the plant had experienced shutdowns, product waste, and numerous acts of sabotage and violence. Walton recognized that the plant was not keeping up with the "evolving expectations of American workers" and worried that these "would increasingly come in conflict with the demands, conditions, and rewards of conventional organizations" like General Foods.[4]

It is tempting to look back to the early 20th century for parallels, and surely some exist. But the disequilibrium at General Foods was not quite like that of Ford Motor and other manufacturers that generations earlier had turned to assembly lines. In those cases, worker unrest was a product of technological change and associated faulty management ideas. General Foods was also struggling in the face of transformation, but in this case, the transformation was primarily social. The 1960s had taken their toll on old models of work, and, as Walton saw it, employees increasingly expected "challenge and personal growth," "egalitarian treatment," and "more attention to the emotional aspects of organization life."[5] Conversely, they were less motivated by competition and material rewards than were their predecessors. Employees of course still wanted to be paid decently, but they also were driven by the "intrinsic interest of the work itself, the human dignity afforded by management, and the social responsibility reflected in the organization's products."[6]

The formal organization had not caught up. It was characterized by simplified tasks with few opportunities for worker development, strict hierarchies and status differentials, rational management with little appreciation for the emotional elements of work, and an emphasis on competition. The organization's payment scheme also failed to reward workers with the nonmaterial benefits they wanted. To Walton, who was a passionate student of Henderson, Mayo, and Roethlisberger, it was obvious that, until the formal organization was brought into alignment with the plant's informal social system, disequilibrium would persist and with it worker discontent and accompanying productivity losses.

When Walton shared his diagnoses with Lyman Ketchum, the operations manager of the Kankakee plant, he found a likeminded ally within General Foods. Walton and Ketchum teamed up on a rather brazen plan: General Foods was preparing to open a new pet food facility in Topeka, Kansas, and the two men saw an opportunity to design the plant from the ground up in ways that would be responsive to employee expectations, improve the quality of working life, and hopefully thereby increase productivity as well. During a 1968 meeting of General Foods managers, Walton and Ketchum pitched their idea for the new plant. They warned that the undertaking "would require turning upside down much of the conventional wisdom of the fields of industrial engineering, accounting, personnel, and the theory of the functional organization."[7] As it turns out, General Foods was game for trying something new.

Over the next several years, Walton worked with the Topeka plant manager, Ed Dulworth, and three of his team to design a pet-food plant from scratch. "My managerial colleagues knew how to produce dog food but had not given much explicit thought to basically alternate forms of social organization and were only partly acquainted with the potentially relevant behavioral sciences," Walton wrote. "Since the profile of my expertise was exactly the opposite [of the plant managers'], it was logical that I would play a major role in providing new inputs and direction in the thinking."[8]

But Walton knew better than to lecture his managerial colleagues. Drawing on his training in social psychology, he recognized that the people around him were more likely to absorb novel concepts if they already had concrete experience in which to contextualize those concepts. In other words, Walton knew that

> [Managers] do not act on new ideas on the basis of the amount of social science evidence (research findings or elaborate theorizing). Rather they act on the basis of the face validity of the idea, that is, its intuitive appeal to them and whether it is in line with some experience of their own.[9]

In short, managers do well with walking sticks.

With this in mind, Walton and the Topeka plant bosses made numerous visits to other sites experimenting with organizational innovation, observed plant culture there, and talked with workers and supervisors. Only once the General Foods staff had these experiences did Walton introduce the "jargon used to describe them and the theories used to rationalize them."[10] Indeed, the learning process of the design team—collaborative, innovative, utilizing behavioral science research—represented a major contribution of the Topeka research.

So, what exactly did this design team do? They started by reimaging the notion of a factory wholesale. The Kankakee plant was a machine—the factory as mechanism. The Topeka plant would be Hendersonian: an organic system. The principal unit of this system would be not the individual or the division but the small team. From the work of Mayo, Roethlisberger, and Homans—and from his own experience and observation—Walton had learned that groups afforded members social satisfaction and individual identification. The team environment overcame differences of individual history, providing a locus of shared goals and norms, while also encouraging independent judgment at the group level. While workers in the Kankakee plant performed fragmented, simplified jobs that could be easily measured and monitored by supervisors, in the Topeka plant, workers would take part in self-managing teams responsible for a set of interconnected tasks.[11]

Minimizing status differentials was another key component of the new Topeka plant. Decades of human relations research showed that the kinds of rigid hierarchy on display in Kankakee were another driver of worker alienation, so Topeka would look different. To this end, the sets of tasks assigned to each group were designed to be equally challenging, and status symbols typical of conventional work organizations—assigned parking spots, separate entrances—were omitted. "My understanding of social psychology suggested to me that differences in formal status and power tend to limit open communication and the development of trust," Walton wrote, "two attributes which are crucial to our division-of-labor scheme and to the leadership pattern we wanted to promote."[12] The self-managing nature of the teams also served to flatten hierarchy and increase autonomy by locating decision making at the lowest feasible level.

When it came to redesigning the pay system, Walton found that he had "run out of theory."[13] Two contrasting theories on the subject produced a practical dilemma. On the one hand, following a rigid, formal protocol focused on quantifiable worker output would reduce the level of subjective judgment exercised by team leaders, minimizing the social distance between leaders and operators. On the other hand, giving team leaders discretion would enable them to evaluate workers more holistically, but at the risk of introducing greater distance between the rank and file and their supervisors, who would be in the position of passing judgment on their subordinate colleagues. So, Walton and the design team discarded both theories and proceeded by trial and error. They would, in a word, test. Trying various options, they ended up with a payment system that rewarded the mastery of an increasing proportion of jobs within the team and within the total plant.

The Topeka plant experiment turned out to be a genuine success, and it received a good deal of deserved attention from academics and practitioners alike. A 1974 study of the plant found "high levels of worker participation, freedom to communicate, expressions of warmth, minimization of status distinction, human dignity, commitment, and individual self-esteem."[14] But what about the bottom line, you ask? These human improvements saved the plant an estimated half million dollars per year.

"As a social psychological consultant, I helped a client solve its problem in a socially responsible way," Walton reflected.[15] His approach was innovative—an application of the medical model, but with a more robust theoretical background, thanks to the years of research separating him from Henderson and Mayo. Walton developed a method of organizational research centered on the reciprocal relationship between social theory and social change.

Walton called this method "action research." Social change—observed through consulting and case development—provided substance for the development of social theory. Theory, in turn, could be used to promote change in action, providing feedback used to revise the theory, and so on. Reflecting on the role of business students and scholars, he explained, "I wanted everybody to think hard about practice—people who are actually working out in the field—how they would use things, as well as how academics would appreciate the knowledge."[16] Action research represented the oscillation between inductive and deductive processes, or, as he put it, an "iterative pattern of acting to conceptualizing to practicing to theorizing about social processes."[17] Armed with real-world, in the field research, iterative testing could improve practices. This was an important elaboration of the medical model, one that recognized that in the years since the founding of human-relations research, much useful knowledge had accrued. Yet all of it remained open to revision in light of the phenomena.

What Managers and Leaders Do

In 1970 John Kotter came to HBS, where he finished his doctorate in a record year-and-a-half. He spent a semester of the doctoral program in a one-on-one reading tutorial with Roethlisberger, who by this time was very much an elder statesman but still eager to pass down the intellectual values of the human relations tradition. Paul Lawrence was another major influence, ensuring that Kotter learned from the best that human relations had to offer.

All of Kotter's research demonstrated his appetite for facts, sense of adventure, and down-to-earth practicality. Kotter's first project, inspired by his longstanding interest in government, was a study of mayors as the managers of cities. How did they do it? What were they like? He and Lawrence coauthored the 1974 book *Mayors in Action*, which drew on extensive fieldwork to identify the critical variables affecting urban leaders. (One particularly striking interview was with Martin Luther King Sr.

at the Ebenezer Baptist Church on the subject of Ivan Allen, who had been the mayor of Atlanta during the 1960s.) Based on Kotter's extensive interviews with mayors, as well as data collected about each city's organizational, social, and economic context, the book argued that mayoral behavior was best understood through an equilibrium model: the system of local government would adjust until various relevant factors—a mayor's personal characteristics, agenda, and ability to mobilize critical resources, as well as those contextual elements—were harmoniously aligned with each other.[18]

Kotter's next study asked a similar question, but in the business context: What do effective managers actually do? Even in the 1970s, hardly anyone had asked this question. The only books on the subject were Sune Carlson's *Executive Behavior* (1951) and Henry Mintzberg's *The Nature of Managerial Work* (1973), which, as Kotter observes in his own introduction, Mintzberg himself admitted "exposes perhaps one percent of the proverbial iceberg."[19] That was enough to get Kotter's attention, though. Mintzberg's skepticism toward standard business school curricula—which held that management was essentially uniform across companies and industries and was centered on command-and-control—had Kotter wondering. Were MBA students really being equipped for their vocation?

Kotter undertook six years of in-depth research on top-level managers in their natural environments. In the first year, he followed 15 managers from nine companies, each for about a month, observing them at work, conducting interviews, and taking up to 100 pages of notes per day. He also visited their homes and asked them about their childhood, education, family life, career history, and job satisfaction. Kotter was present for the dramatic and the mundane: "If the [manager] was just sitting at his desk reading his mail," Kotter noted, "I was there too."[20] The result of this time-intensive process was a textured picture of managers' actual behavior, something that could not be captured by a questionnaire, which was the most popular approach to field research at the time.

Kotter spent the next two years wrestling with the mass of data he had collected, searching for regularities (Henderson's "uniformities") within the complexity. He noticed that all of the managers relied on two mechanisms: their agenda—which included what they needed to accomplish, in what order, and how long it would take—and their network of relationships: the people critical to achieving their desired ends. The success of the managers varied and depended on the effective navigation of the social complexities of those networks. The particular behaviors involved in social navigation might appear inefficient or illogical to an uninformed observer, but actually those behaviors followed a compelling logic once one understood the human challenges managers faced. As a human relations specialist, trained in the medical model's methods of listening and observation, Kotter could see what other so-called management experts failed to.

Bottom line, Kotter's effective managers were not all alike, as orthodoxy insisted. They weren't just agenda-keepers who ordered subordinates around. Instead, they exhibited diverse behaviors and possessed no singular attribute that predicted success, save for their ability to adapt to the demands of the job and the characters and capacities of their subordinates. One of Kotter's case studies drives home the point, as he discusses two managers leading different parts of the same large company: "Fred," who had a clear-cut agenda and authoritative style in managing a large sales force, and "Ren," who was laid back, humorous, and who, as head of an engineering department responsible for product development, tended to be more personal and interactive with his subordinates. Yet both Fred and Ren were able to accomplish their goals.

The book that emerged from this study, *The General Managers* (1982), argued that the rational, dispassionate manager, controlling subordinates from afar according to a general body of principles applicable in all circumstances, was a fiction. "Perhaps the single most fundamental finding arising from this study," Kotter wrote, "is that these effective executives were significantly dissimilar in a large number of important dimensions— regarding who they are, what they do, why they behave that way—from the dominant conception today of the effective 'professional manager.'"[21] Seemingly, every successful manager needed a clear agenda and a reliable network, but how they mobilized that network in service of that agenda varied widely.

Further revisionist research followed naturally. A prevailing notion among business scholars was that leaders differed from managers in a crucial way: the former were innovative, creative, and inspiring, while the latter were task-oriented, unimaginative, and mechanical. The sense was that leadership was essentially good and management essentially bad, and so executives should strive to be leaders rather than managers. Kotter tested this conventional wisdom through another round of intensive fieldwork. This time he surveyed and interviewed even more people—hundreds of executives. Again, he recorded extensive observational notes.

After analyzing patterns in the data, he arrived at a new insight: neither leadership nor management was essentially good or bad, and successful organizations possessed the right combination of both. According to Kotter's research, leadership was best thought of as "a process that helps direct and mobilize people and/or their ideas" in pursuit of change, while management's task was to ensure that organizational goals—including changes sought by leadership—were pursued on time and on budget.[22] Thus management and leadership supported each other, and both had an important function in complex organizations: "Strong management without much leadership can turn bureaucratic and stifling, producing order for order's sake. Strong leadership without much management can become messianic and cult-like, producing change for change's sake."[23] Effective organizations were those that were able to find an equilibrium between the two modes. Self-evidently, this precluded a top-down prescription applicable to all in common circumstances and encouraged continuous, on-the-ground experimenting—testing—to arrive at individual optimizations.

The research was described in *A Force for Change* (1990), which was published by a major press and was widely read by managers and academics—something that can't be said for many books of theoretically driven, abstract business scholarship. For managers, the book provided a conceptual frame that would help put knowledge into action. "I was interested in doing something that might contribute in some way to improve life on earth," Kotter told me at one point. "My focus was always on reality, as best as I could understand it."[24]

Taking Charge

Eventually, Kotter moved on from academia to full-time consulting, but the themes of his work seeded future scholarship. He brought the human relations paradigm to bear on two new subjects—leadership and change—that proved fruitful areas of investigation for his colleagues.

Among them was John "Jack" Gabarro, another inquisitive scholar with a nose for important questions. I was chair of Gabarro's dissertation committee at HBS and collaborated with him on case-writing. Before coming to HBS, he had served as a lieutenant in the U.S. Army field artillery, a tour of duty that left him hard of hearing in one ear after he stood too close to a cannon. Ironically, the course he taught most often was a second-year elective, Interpersonal Behavior, which focused on listening skills. Under Gabarro's guidance, the course, a successor to the original Human Relations course taught by Roethlisberger, was hugely popular, attracting as many as 500 second-year students from a class of typically around 800.

Alongside teaching, Gabarro did painstaking field investigations into organizational relationships at moments of disequilibrium. In particular, in the course of conducting executive education seminars and consulting with clients, he had developed an interest in changes in command. What happens when a new manager takes charge, with the goal of solving some problem of organizational design? Following the methods of his HBS predecessors, Gabarro broke the big question down into smaller ones, the better to guide his listening and observation programs. What stages of learning characterized this transition? What organizational and interpersonal dynamics affected managers' effectiveness in their new role? What managerial behaviors distinguished failures from successes? These were all questions seeking answers that would have important implications for practice.

In order to gather data on the phenomenon of taking charge, Gabarro conducted three sets of field studies on 17 management successions, some successful and some less so. These studies, pursued over eight years, consisted of longitudinal analyses of contemporary managerial successions as well as relevant historical case studies. Gabarro used the contemporary and historical findings to examine distinct periods of the transition, an inductive approach that echoed the methodology of the Hawthorne studies. Like Kotter's study of managers, Gabarro's prolonged immersion in the material lent his results depth, texture, and force.

From this research, Gabarro came to understand taking charge as "the process by which a manager establishes mastery and influence in a new assignment."[25] While Gabarro observed that managers achieved mastery and influence in very different ways and used different skills depending on the particular environment, he also saw consistencies in the mass of data, realizing that each case of management transition tended to unfold in a common sequence of five stages. These stages, which are described in detail in Gabarro's 1987 book *The Dynamics of Taking Charge*, include Taking Hold, Immersion, Reshaping, Consolidation, and Refinement. By the end of this process, which typically took two-and-a-half to three years, the successful managers Gabarro observed had achieved both expertise and impact.

Gabarro identified the new managers' prior experiences and interpersonal relationships as keys to the success or failure of the transitions he studied. Successful managers had relevant experience, were able to cultivate productive relationships with new colleagues, subordinates, and superiors and to accurately assess the organization and its problems in a timely way, building a management team centered on shared expectations and problem-solving. Those lacking experience and less able to build relationships were liable to succumb to what Gabarro called the "Lone Ranger Syndrome"—a solitary style less likely to lead to correct diagnoses or effective solutions.[26] Like Kotter, he found that relationships were at the heart of managerial effectiveness.

Also like Kotter, Gabarro concluded that the image of the one-size-fits-all manager was more fiction than fact. Rather, the competencies associated with effective managers, both experiential and interpersonal, were highly contingent upon the organization and its particular problems. After eight years of acquainting himself with actual managers, he wrote that "the all-purpose general manager who can be slotted into just about any organization, function, or industry exists only in management textbooks."[27]

The Mind of a Manager

Managerial life has also been a dominant interest of Linda Hill, whose research at HBS on management and leadership is responsible for major contributions to the field. After completing undergraduate work in psychology and a PhD in Behavioral Sciences at the University of Chicago, Hill took up a post-doctorate position at HBS, pursuing a number of research projects, including a longitudinal study of MBAs, which she performed with John Kotter.[28] Her postdoctoral year also coincided with the deregulation of the U.S. financial industry in the early 1980s, and she became interested in looking at how banks were retraining people to work in a vastly changed environment.

Hill officially joined the HBS faculty in 1984. When she began to teach MBAs, she had an epiphany: despite having read much about what management was, she did not know how to actually help MBAs learn to do the job.[29] The limited literature on transition to a managerial position treated it as an event rather than a process. (This was before Gabarro had published his own research laying out the five stages of management transition, though Hill would also take an approach that differed from her colleague's and that reached different insights.) Furthermore, management theory ignored the subjective experiences of managers as well as the social and psychological consequences of those experiences—exactly what her training in psychology and behavioral science had prepared her to explore.[30]

In the spirit of the early HBS researchers, Hill embarked on a field study. "The phenomenon of interest nearly always dictates the methodology for studying it," she wrote in *Becoming a Manager*, the 1992 book describing her research.[31]

Because this research was focused on "how" and "why" questions about contemporary events, it seemed that a qualitative field study was the logical approach. I collected any data, qualitative or quantitative, which came my way. I relied on observation, formal interviews and informal conversations (in the hallways, at meals, during breaks in formal meetings), well- and ill-informed informants, and archival and published materials. The primary sources of data were semi-structured interviews and unstructured observations. As the research progressed and patterns seemed to form, I probed more deeply the issues that appeared to dominate and to question more precisely and make more focused observations.[32]

This was pure Hawthorne-type stuff. So were the questions she posed—revelatory, basic questions that no one had thought to ask: "What do new managers find most challenging? How do they learn to be managers? On what resources, individual and organizational, do they rely?"[33]

In search of answers, Hill followed 19 managers at two firms through their first year in the role. The fieldwork involved three years (1985 to 1988) of periodic visits with the managers, during which Hill spent hours at a time interviewing them and their subordinates and observing the managers in their daily environment. Her approach was like that of a physician analyzing signs and symptoms to arrive at a diagnosis. In the end, she had more than 2,000 pages of interview and field notes. Her ambition was not to test any particular hypothesis but to stick closely to the experience of new managers, combing through the mountainous pages of field data looking for significant variables and using existing theory as a walking stick to guide the search for meaningful patterns.

At first the search for patterns was not especially fruitful. "Because the research design was longitudinal, one of my first endeavors was to search for periodicity in the data," she wrote. "Much to my chagrin, no phases or stages appeared in the new managers' experiences."[34] But then,

> [On] one memorable evening, … it suddenly came to me that the new managers were learning *what* they needed to learn only *when* they needed to learn it. Time was not the organizing principle that would explain my data; problems and surprises would do so. After this insight, the analytical scheme began to fall into place.[35]

What Hill discovered was that becoming a manager involved a transformation of professional identity, from star producer to supervisor. In the process, new managers experienced a sudden onslaught of responsibility—what one manager described as running into a "brick wall."[36] Managers initially expected to exercise formal authority over financial and business matters, with little awareness of the relational aspects of the job. Only when they actually stepped into the role did their expectations of power and control—residues of their formal training—yield to the realities of the workplace, especially the influence of co-workers. One manager who participated in the study compared transitioning to the new role to teaching beginners to ride bicycles—a kind of learning that could never be adequately explained, only experienced. "You can give [beginners] theory," he said, "you can give them a good feel for it, and work on the individual skills. But until they get on the bike and start riding it and fall down a couple of times themselves, they just can't know it."[37]

If managers for that matter, learned what they needed to know only when they needed to know it, then the traditional approach to MBA training needed an overhaul. In *Becoming a Manager*, Hill suggests that such training should inculcate not only functional expertise but also interpersonal skills and an awareness of the changes they will face when they join organizations in professional capacities. Traditionally, MBA classes featured few opportunities for experiential learning, and students were typically left to make the connection between theory and practice on their own.[38] In 1998, Hill dramatically revised HBS's first-year required course in Leadership and Organizational Behavior (LEAD), in an effort to help students "confront both the task learning and the personal learning involved in becoming a manager."[39] The new curriculum was designed around an MBA's "psychological calendar," with classroom exercises that emphasized teamwork and relationships, and that showed students how to apply knowledge taught in the lecture hall to concrete experiences in their lives.[40] The model she created is still the basis of the introductory LEAD course today.

Hill also used concepts from *Becoming a Manager* to coach practitioners. She created the first installments of Harvard ManageMentor, an online arsenal of interactive lessons for managers confronting new situations in real time and applied her insights in executive education courses and her consulting practice. Many of Hill's insights have proven applicable outside the corporate world; in our conversations, she has related to me communications from a Brooklyn priest, a German physician, and a hockey coach, all of whom read *Becoming a Manager* and identified with the experiences described there. The book's second edition, published in 2002, zeroed in on several additional questions most often raised by new managers: how to navigate organizational politics, influence peers and bosses, and develop a diverse team in times of change.[41]

Hill's interest in practice informed her next project, on leadership.[42] In *Being the Boss* (2007), coauthored with business executive Kent Lineback and rooted in the real lives of managers grappling with a journey of transformation, Hill identified three imperatives of leadership: managing yourself, managing your team, and managing your network. Later she took up the topic of innovation, collecting data about what it takes to be an agent of change and writing yet another book, *Collective Genius* (2014). Throughout her career and her many works, she has championed inductive methods as the foundation of conceptual frameworks. "How do we know what we write is true?" she asked in *Being the Boss*. "We know from research and our collective and complementary experiences of managing, teaching, and consulting with literally thousands of managers in diverse organizations and in varied roles from all around the world."[43] Although Hill's research interests have evolved, her methods have always been based on observation and a constant, thoughtful, and open-minded engagement with the field she was studying—a characteristic she shares with Kotter, Gabbaro, Walton, and other scholars researching organizational phenomena, testing her theories and asking and answering questions in the mold of Henderson, Mayo, and Roethlisberger.

White-Collar Schoolmasters

While my colleagues in Organizational Behavior were pursuing these paths, I had changed the direction of my research from its earlier focus on plastics and innovations to trying to understand a growing new industry made up of companies that provided professional services to their clients, firms that offered expertise in the areas of accounting, advertising, executive search, information technology, investment banking, law, and management consulting. I had earlier begun to do what my HBS colleagues did, consulting to companies with organizational issues that needed fixing. For me the opportunities originally clustered in financial firms like Citicorp, Morgan Stanley, and Goldman Sachs, and from this grew my interest in understanding how professional service companies were organized and functioned. In the late 1990s I was introduced to Tom Tierney, who was at the time the CEO of Bain and Company, and he and I decided to collaborate on trying to understand how and why professional service firms were organized as they were. We were particularly interested in how these firms went about developing and keeping talented employees, whose performance was fundamental to the success of the firm, employees whom we called "stars" in the book, *Aligning the Stars*, that came out of our collaboration.

Following the medical model, we began by interviewing senior managers about their problems in developing and keeping new talent. We also spent time in each of the organizations we were studying, learning to understand who their clients were, what services they provided, whom they hired, and how they developed their talents. Our walking stick was the notion that successful professional firms had to bring in young people whose goals, talents, and interests fit with the firm's strategies. We determined that for a professional service firm to become and remain successful, the firm's leaders had to focus on aligning the firm's strategies, organization (including "people systems"), culture and leadership with the aim of developing, teaching, and motivating the "stars" of a company to perform and to feel invested in the company.

Equally important was alignment. Once stated, this sounds a truism worthy of a fortune cookie: organizations that align their myriad efforts are more likely to succeed. Yet, it is routinely observable within organizations and at the level of business news reporting, that some companies, some organizations, fail precisely because of an inability to align common efforts across multiple individuals and departments. To take but one example: a law firm that penalizes its partners for high turnover can become, and in one case we studied in fact became, a firm with zero turnover and rising mediocrity. Alignment is hard to achieve precisely "because the environment in which organizations compete and serve customers is constantly changing. New services and competitive approaches can require changes in organization."[44] To compete, in other words, organizations need to test to optimize change.

Alignment is, and remains, a systems challenge. Four aspects of the firm—strategy, organization, culture, and leadership—are the frame of the choices being made by leadership and that professionals are tasked with implementing day by day. As *Aligning the Stars* laid out, within the professional service firms we studied, meeting this challenge was an exercise of informed adaptability and a relentless focus on questions as well as answers. Identifying the most important factors that contribute to alignment, and success, was a starting point. As we articulated in its opening pages:

> No book can offer its readers customized answers to all the particular decisions they and their organizations face. But good books can prompt their readers to *pursue* the *few* questions that really matter. Ultimately, success depends on saying *no* to pressing but inconsequential questions, while concentrating your energy on those few questions that will determine your firm's destiny and your own.[45]

Years later, I agree with every word. However, I would now emphasize how and why these observations are examples of the larger medical model approach to understanding organizational behavior. Observing and listening, or devising our walking stick for researching the firms at the center of *Aligning the Stars*, was the first task. Accumulating the resulting data, the insights into practices at firms succeeding and failing, was the result. Gleaning from that data a formalized but adaptable method of testing the efficacy of a firm's practices—testing its ability to align—was the result. Decades after HBS's pioneers first articulated and later refined the medical model, here it was applied to solve the practical problems confronting professional service firms, their clients and employees, and the wider world with which all of them interacted.

CHAPTER 5

Where Are We Today?

In the late 20th and early 21st centuries important research in human relations using the medical model—research performed on location with consequences for real businesses—has continued, and we will be looking at some of these studies in the first half of this chapter, notably my own research on boards of directors, Jack Gabarro and David Thomas' work on minority executives in the corporate world, and Tsedal Neeley's work on the linguistic challenges facing global companies. Unfortunately, the same period has also seen a change in the kind of research business schools consider important and choose to focus on. The field of human relations has become decidedly unfashionable within the academy and has been largely superseded by numeric studies focusing on numbers and statistics rather than on real-time human behavior. Thus, we will conclude this chapter with a look at the work of the quants and a discussion of why I believe its increased prominence is so worrisome.

Boards of Directors

In 1983 I was asked to join the board of directors of the Brunswick corporation, the oldest publicly listed company in Chicago. I agreed to do so, not least because it would give me a new perspective on publicly listed corporations and their ownership, about which I knew very little. My impression at the time was that boards, while important, were largely dominated by management, including the company's CEO. A few years later, in 1987, I was asked to join the board of a second company, the Sandy Corporation. It was a family-controlled company, but one also listed publicly. Sandy provided marketing services and advice to the major automotive manufacturers in Detroit, especially Ford and General Motors.

As I attended board meetings at both Brunswick and Sandy, I did what came naturally to me, I listened and observed the discussions in the board meetings, and as I learned more about the companies and the issues they were facing, I became more active in the discussions. In retrospect, I realized that I had used the medical model to observe how these two boards were functioning and the differences between them. As I listened to the proceedings, my instinctive use of the medical model had helped me understand the functioning of each board with regards to who were the leaders and who were the most and least effective directors in influencing the discussions. I also found myself considering how well the chair and/or the CEO allowed independent directors to contribute to the discussions and influence decisions. In essence, while serving as a director, I kept the medical model constantly at the back of my mind informing my actions and piquing my interest in learning more about how boards functioned and the role they really played in a company's decision making.

Eventually, encouraged by Marty Lipton, the managing partner of Wachtel, Lipton, Rosen, and Katz, whom I met through a council of competitiveness established by Congress, I undertook a research project looking into the functioning of corporate boards and how well they performed in the United States, the United Kingdom, and Germany, the last of which had a unique system that included worker participation, which I felt was of particular interest. To do so, my research associate and I first sent out a paper and pencil questionnaire (this was during the days when the Internet was just coming into its own), to 800 board members of U.S. public companies, whom we selected based on company size and industry. After we sent and received completed questionnaires from a statistically significant percent of the directors, my research associate traveled to meet personally with many of them, giving us the opportunity for one-on-one interviews covering their experiences on the boards on which they served.

Soon after we finished collecting the data, I attended a second meeting of the competitiveness committee, this time in Washington DC. Again, I met with Marty Lipton, and we agreed on two things: first to write an article aimed at improving the functioning of boards and meant for readers who themselves were serving on boards; and, second, more immediately to share a taxi back to the airport after the meeting, where we would talk about the details of the article.

On that ride to the airport, we agreed quickly on the general focus of the article: (1) keep the board as small as possible, but make sure that it represented shareholders; (2) have an independent leader, the "lead director" as we called the position, on the board in addition to the CEO and the chairman of the board. This lead director would be selected by the independent directors from among their number and his or her duties would be to hold and lead a meeting of only the independent directors at the time of each regular board meeting. The purpose of this meeting would be to collect the concerns and ideas from the independent directors, and the lead director would then have the responsibility to communicate these ideas to the CEO and chair.

The article was published in the *Business Lawyer* in November 1992, and I later followed it with my book, *Pawns or Potentates: The realities of America's corporate boards.*[1] It gradually gained a large readership and influenced the way many boards functioned, in particular reducing the dominance of the CEO and management directors. In this regard, it seems to have given the outside directors more input into the agenda and content of the board meetings and the actual discussion in the board room. In essence we enhanced the power and influence of the independent directors, and in doing so contributed, I think I can say, to the increased effectiveness of boards in the United States and perhaps elsewhere.

Minority Executives

With the passage of time, the medical model was increasingly adapted to the purpose of raising questions concerning minorities and management. Among the very first such endeavors that aimed to understand the leadership qualities of the most successful minority managers was the work of two HBS colleagues, David Thomas and John Gabarro, who conducted a field study, described in their 1999 book *Breaking Through*, that found African American executives who reached upper levels of management encountered and overcame barriers to promotion throughout their careers that their white counterparts did not.[2] For many readers, this was probably not news. But it was important to specify these barriers. It was also significant how these barriers were identified. The fieldwork took three years, included interviews with almost 250 individuals, and the review of thousands of pages of transcripts. As described in the opening pages of their book, the 54 executives and managers studied were subjects of

> Six to fifteen hours interviewing each person on topics such as family background, progression of jobs, development as a manager, experience of race and its effects on career, and the events and relationships seen as critical to current level of career attainment.[3]

Through the extensive and rigorous use of the medical model, Thomas and Gabarro identified individual and organizational factors that enabled minority executives to rise in their companies.

Global Perspectives

In 2010 the CEO of the Japanese e-commerce firm, Rakuten, made the decision to change the company's working language from Japanese to English, despite the fact that many of the company's 10,000 or so employees were Japanese. My colleague, Tsedal Neeley, spent five years observing how this change was realized and how the company's culture and its employees were affected by it, publishing the results in her 2019 book, *The Language of Global Success*.[4] Using the medical model she listened, observed, and tested her theories. In her introduction, Neeley described the access, granted her by Rakuten's CEO, Hiroshi Mikitani, as follows:

> Throughout the study, Mikitani granted me total access to his company, inviting me to go anywhere in the world to talk to any of his employees without imposing a single condition. I talked with people as many times as I deemed necessary to develop a rich understanding of the lingua franca and cultural phenomena as they unfolded in real time.[5]

Extensive interviews of 650 employees across the company's many international offices in Europe, Asia, North and South America revealed that employees making the change from Japanese to English could be divided into three categories, those that felt they had become expats in their own country, those that were native English speakers who felt that the change in language brought unexpected cultural challenges with it and those who were neither native Japanese nor English speakers and had therefore the easiest time with adjusting to the new practices. Neeley was able to use this information to help the company improve the implementation of the new language, and this advice has been translated to other international companies making the same change. In other words, her work is yet another example of how human relations and the medical model can still be used to provide relevant, practical answers to real-world challenges faced by today's companies.

The World of the Quants

The present academic universe, so different from the one inhabited and created by Donham, Henderson, Mayo, and Roethlisberger, is the product of decades of concerted efforts to "professionalize" business schools and introduce to them a rigor that supposedly was previously lacking. As early as 1954, Roethlisberger lamented that human relations was becoming a "dirty word" in academic circles.[6] What happened was the arrival of the "*enfants terribles*," as Roethlisberger called them: social scientists housed in traditional academic departments who began flocking to business schools, bringing "models about man and systems of all sorts."[7] These scholars were far more interested in the emerging fields of game theory and decision analysis than in interpersonal communication or field methodology.[8] Their shiny new rationalistic approaches relied on novel computational and statistical methods that "made human relations theory sound old-fashioned."[9]

The usual complaint among these economists and sociologists was that human relations was nonscientific—beneath the exacting and objective standards of the quantitative behavioral sciences. Some thought us medical model practitioners misguided in more basic ways: either we were pawns of power-hungry executives or we were enemies of reason, duty, and hard work. The sociologist Daniel Bell, one of the fiercest opponents of human relations, published a widely read essay accusing us of blindly accepting management's own conception of workers as means to economic ends and of manipulating workers into submission. "The belief in man as an end in himself has been ground under by the machine, and the social science of the factory researchers is not a science of man, but a cow-sociology," he wrote in 1947.[10]

Even from within HBS itself, criticism of this sort was heard. Already in 1957, marketing professor Malcolm McNair disparaged human relations for being too "soft" and sentimental and for encouraging these characteristics in MBA students, who had no use for the study of human beings as such. In a lecture and article titled "What Price Human Relations?" McNair considered our work a "fad," "amateur psychiatry," and based in the sort of skill that need not be analyzed and taught because it was a natural product of "breeding, home, church, education, and experience generally."[11] Taking matters to another level, he raged that:

> Too much emphasis on human relations encourages people to feel sorry for themselves, makes it easier for them to slough off responsibility, to find excuses for failure, to act like children .... In these respects, the cult of human relations is but part and parcel of the sloppy sentimentalism characterizing the world today.[12]

McNair's position was characteristic of the moment. The early Cold War academic environment was suffused with "hard-nosed" rationalism, an approach credited with supporting the Allied industrial program that enabled victory in World War II and which was seen as essential to national security in the nuclear age. Decision theory, for example, was a side effect of the atomic bomb, a method for thinking coolly about the otherwise-terrifying problem of mutually assured destruction. And this thinking could now be done with the aid of computers, which had made significant advances during the war for purposes of cryptography and modeling nuclear chain reactions. So-called rigor was not only desirable, it was also now possible, thanks to new tools.

In particular, this desire was felt by two groups of people. One was academic social scientists, especially economists, for whom business schools provided opportunities for academic careerism. This is not to suggest that the outsiders who flocked to business schools were other than sincere in their interests and their efforts; however, the effect of their take-over of business education was its reinvention as a traditional academic field, in which success is measured in publications and citations, not in real-world impact. The other party responsible for the transformation of business schools was the Ford Foundation, which sank millions of dollars into programs that professed a more scientific approach. These programs became havens for the quants—scholars who crunched numbers, used statistics, and developed elaborate theories from their offices—rather than empiricists who went into the field to listen, observe, and test.

The deep irony is that business schools welcomed quants with the goal of achieving greater relevance, and in doing so created a field that grew increasingly insular, obsessed with mathematical models so elaborate that hardly anyone can understand them. Whereas human relations offers an effective bridge between scholarship and practice, quantitative business studies alienate practitioners with impenetrable jargon and equations. Henderson's walking stick, which to the organizational behaviorist was much akin to the doctor's stethoscope and tongue depressor, and the skilled experience of a diagnostician has given way to methodologies that undermine their own contributions by oversimplifying the complexities of real people and organizations.

The linguistic inscrutability of much recent research is a natural consequence of these kinds of methodologies that keep scholars at a distance from the phenomena they study. The gap between investigators and the objects of their investigation produces ironies: researchers who study corporate boards but have never been in a boardroom, who analyze organizational effectiveness from a computer in a cubicle, and who use a scholarly vocabulary that is Greek to the average reader.[13]

A 2018 article on workplace loneliness offers a case in point.[14] The question it addresses is an important one that goes back to Walton's studies of worker alienation and Mayo's exploration of worker sentiments and social relations. But the method illustrates how sophisticated quantitative analysis can go astray. The reliance on prior theory and "mediator–moderator" analysis to build a causal link between loneliness and poor job performance ends up masking the question of interest behind a nearly impenetrable screen of academic jargon and complicated math.[15] The article's authors rely on a questionnaire that asks whether respondents agree with terse statements like "I feel left out of this organization." The yeses and nos that result are amenable to quantification, but occlude the expression of underlying motivations and emotions. (You'll remember that this kind of directed questioning was discarded by the Hawthorne researchers in favor of open-ended interviews more likely to reveal a worker's "total situation.") By curtailing responses, such scripted surveys end up producing an abstraction, "the lonely worker," rather than a living portrait of individuals.

How accurate is this paint-by-numbers worker and how valid is the analysis of their loneliness? The authors themselves note that their theory could be flawed: the causal arrow might point in the opposite direction, from poor job performance to increasing loneliness and decreasing commitment to the organization.[16] And perhaps the cause of poor performance lies in personality traits or personal events like divorce or the death of a loved one, but rather than explore these issues, the authors control "trait negative affectivity" and "private-life loneliness" out of existence. [17] These may be the very things they're looking for in their search for causes! Which comes first, poor performance or workplace loneliness? This research cannot tell us, but it looks complicated and it's methodology rigorous, so it found a publisher.

This sort of research is hardly the worst of it. At the very least, the authors recognize the limitations of their case. And while they sacrifice meaning on the altar of statistics, one can at least make heads or tails of what they say and subject it to critique. Less can be said of another article, published that same year in the *Academy of Management Journal.* This article, on "LMX differentiation," uses the coded language typical of most journal articles. With the stated purpose of offering insight into leader–membership exchange in work groups (what does that really mean?), the article presents its conclusions in highly technical jargon:

The estimated true-score relationships showed (a) the relationship between LMX differentiation and group performance was not significant ($k = 24$, $\rho = .01$, 90% CI [$-.06$, $.03$]), (b) a significant negative relationship between LMX differentiation and emergent states ($k = 21$, $r\rho = -.32$, 90% CI [$-.32$, $-.17$]), and (c) a significant negative relationship between LMX differentiation and group processes ($k = 18$, $\rho = -.35$, 90% CI [$-.38$, $-.21$])."[18]

Imagine that you are a business leader confronting a real-time management challenge within your work groups and are given this article from which to glean a solution. Very few practitioners have the time or energy to unearth a usable insight from language like this.

Numbers can also mislead and distort. Despite airtight calculations and sophisticated modeling, the imposition of a wished-for meaning on raw data and the neglect of social and relational context may result in faulty inferences and unintended consequences. Consider Michael Jensen's 1976 "Theory of the Firm," one of the rare academic-theory articles that has been influential, establishing so-called agency theory as a dominant paradigm of business.[19] According to Jensen's theory, there is a keystone concept of shareholder power. Managers are simply agents of that power, which serves to maximize shareholder wealth. All this boils down to a complex equation that accommodates "non-pecuniary" factors, including such things as carpeting, air-conditioning, and, in something of a leap, personal relations like "love" and "respect" (Jensen's quotes).[20] Basically, Jensen's equation for making the most money possible, in pursuit of increasing shareholder power, quantifies the human factor along with the carpeting. As a theory, it's elegant: a single outcome against which to measure every aspect of an organization, with the promise of optimizing efficiency. It also obviates the need to observe, listen and test. Why undertake any such efforts when an organization's efforts can be distilled to one elegant outcome?

If the consequences of abandoning the walking stick for what we might call rocking-chair scholarship were confined within the halls of academia, we could restrict our lament to lost opportunities rather than active injury. But, as has become apparent in the wake of Jensen's theory, ivory-tower theorizing can have real-world consequences that compound rather than resolve organizational difficulties. In practice, shareholder power, also termed shareholder capitalism, though generating huge profits for a few, has led to less-than-happy outcomes, including the decline of long-term strategies for growth, an upsurge in short-selling as investors seek immediate profits, and the destruction of companies with significant value.

Yet another problem for contemporary management scholars over-enamored with quantitative methodology is that it yields diminishing returns. The theoretical territory dictated by journal criteria is already thoroughly plowed. The more "mature" the body of theory, the more likely that current research will involve modifications or elaborations of existing studies, resulting in ever smaller findings—or as one of my colleagues calls it, "pistol shots instead of cannon balls."[21] The LMX article mentioned previously is an example of this kind of research: a meta-analysis of published studies, proposing to resolve a paradox evident in prior research: that leader–membership exchange is effective in enhancing individual performance but detrimental to group performance.[22] Using an "equity–equality framework," the researchers conclude that, for managers, there is a trade-off between using merit to differentiate among workers (those selected are more productive) and using egalitarian principles (the group is more productive). The study ends up yielding only minor amendments to established theory and leaves out the personal factors that may have influenced workers' reactions to both equity and equality.[23]

The meta-analysis of large datasets has also become a popular approach, given that such studies are much less costly than multiyear field studies involving observation and interviews. In some instances, such analyses are well-suited to the topic. For example, an article about the evaluation of innovation by brokerage firms uses a dataset from the medical device-industry, "an innovation-intensive context," to analyze the negative reaction of outside organizations (brokerage firms, media) to companies engaging in the production of new knowledge.[24] Another study, of the influence of short sellers on firm growth, uses a longitudinal dataset (2000–2014) to analyze trends in managerial reactions to the danger posed by activist shareholders.[25] Both studies use large datasets effectively, to provide illuminating aerial views of the organizational landscape.

The emphasis on this type of research has resulted in a crisis in business education and scholarship that has only intensified in recent years. Especially during the last couple of decades, we've lost talent. I've seen colleagues throw up their hands and walk away, taking jobs in other sectors where they feel they can make a difference. I know junior scholars who, under the publish-or-perish dictate, check boxes for advancement by solving narrow, academic problems. And I know editors who experience the publish-or-perish problem from the opposite end of the gun, caught between esoteric scholarship or solutionless-but-digestible business publishing "lite." I've seen a sense of paralysis and cynicism take hold.

Even against repeated waves of criticism, business research has remained stubbornly insignificant. Almost 30 years ago, during the 1993 meeting of the Academy of Management, the organization's president, Don Hambrick, pointed out that the problem was not going away.

> Each August, we come to talk with each other; during the rest of the year we read each other's papers in our journals and write our own paper so that we may, in turn, have an audience the following August.[26] The Academy, Hambrick concluded, had become "an incestuous, closed loop."[27]

Three decades later little has changed.

I have seen up close the impact of this system on younger scholars. The extremely low rates of acceptance in our field's top journals—less than 5 percent of submissions are accepted—make the first few years in the profession a particularly stressful period for young faculty, whose careers depend on securing a few seemingly arbitrary "hits." As one of my young colleagues reflected:

> I think that most junior faculty today come up with their research agenda largely in retrospect, trying to make sense of the compilation of papers that hit, so that they can tie them all together in a tenure review package.[28]

This is not a formula for effective knowledge-building.

What else has been sacrificed in the pursuit of academic legitimacy? There are certainly financial costs to the research produced in the name of academic showboating and careerism. One study estimated the costs of producing journal articles with no actionable content at around $600 million each year.[29] This money comes from universities and grants, many of which are publicly funded. While $600 million per year is a disturbing number in its own right, the price tag is unconscionably high given the lack of results.

Even less appreciated is the human cost of our current system. Many talented young people are spending their most productive years doing research that even they do not find interesting or important, when instead they could be solving real problems.[30] This opportunity cost becomes even less justifiable when we consider the resources spent educating these young scholars: doctoral education, like research funding, is subsidized by universities and grants. But what are the funders receiving in return? What is a doctoral degree in business worth, if all it does is fortify the echo chamber of scholars conversing with each other?[31]

The immense pressures placed on junior faculty in a publish-or-perish culture come with significant psychological costs to the individual. I have noticed a heightened degree of anxiety and frustration in the voices of my young colleagues when they talk about their research and possibility of promotion. Of course, there is always stress and uncertainty in the early phase of one's career, but these emotions dominate the experience of young faculty who should instead be experiencing the joy and excitement of making real contributions. Several business scholars offered the following advice in a 2007 article:

> Individuals with children and a desire to spend a great deal of time in their children's development need not apply, at least not at prestigious institutions where demands are extremely high … . Family medical history is also a consideration. Histories of heart disease, suppressed immune systems, and other diseases exacerbated by stress are signals that an academic career in organization science may not be the best choice. Long work hours, periods of little sleep, and randomness in key outcomes yield stressful lives. Combining a predisposition for disease with a stressful life is not a good idea.[32]

The language is tongue-in-cheek, but it satirizes an ugly reality.

That new methods and academic approaches are tried out, introduced, and practiced is all for the good, when they work. That old, proven, solution-focused methods and approaches are phased out entirely is not. Amy Edmondson and Stacey McManus have written about methodological fit—different methods appropriate to different phases of theoretical development (mature, intermediate, or nascent) in a given area of investigation. On this view, a nascent theory, applicable to new, unusual, or unknown phenomena, calls for qualitative, exploratory research.[33] It seems to me that the problem with the workplace-loneliness and LMX-differentiation studies is poor methodological fit: abstract quantification and theoretical analysis are awkward tools for investigating psychological and social phenomena better understood through interviews, observations, and extensive engagement in the field.

A case can certainly be made for a variety of methods suited to a variety of topics, but the preference for large datasets usually has little to do with methodologic fitness and much to do with ease and likelihood of publication. During a publishing workshop at the 2018 Academy of Management Conference, a panel of speakers encouraged junior scholars to "make friends who collect data" or to purchase secondary datasets. Such an approach to data collection is the opposite of getting into an organization, gaining intimate familiarity with the phenomena, and discovering relevant patterns—"finding the rat," as Roethlisberger would say. At the end of the publishing session, when an audience member asked to what extent, if ever, panelists consulted practitioners about their research ideas, the panelists had literally nothing to say.

Data-heavy studies appease editors' desire for theoretical sophistication and quantitative rigor (that word, again), particularly in the form of statistically significant T-tests. Qualitative research, meanwhile, is a tough sell: the data are poorly suited to correlational analyses and often require lengthy quotation and explanation extending beyond the page limits of most journals. True, articles featuring inductive research have appeared in the top-tier journals in the past few years, among them articles about knowledge workers in the gig economy, temporary team coordination in hospital emergency rooms, conflict resolution at a U.S. Army mental health post, and professional identity at NASA during a period of innovation.[34] Yet time-intensive investigations remain out of sync with publication cycles and promotion timelines, and cultural biases against "soft" data militate against a broader return to hands-on work.[35]

Notably, and ironically, one subbranch of management scholarship specialization—behavioral economics—has managed to elude public indifference and consequent irrelevance. Ironic because the economists accomplished this feat by doing what HBS' founders did a century ago: admitting psychology and psychologists into their academic midst. The work of two seminal psychologists, Daniel Kahneman and Amos Tversky, introduced the research and insights that three seminal economists, Richard Thaler, Abhijit Banerjee, and Esther Duflo, applied and thereby became Nobel Memorial Prize in Economic Science laureates. They, and other behavioral economic adherents, have also produced numerous bestsellers and have undeniable influence. But while their debts to organizational behavior are clear, they are also clearly partial. As one of the field's most ardent critics, Gerd Gigerenzer notes, actual people living actual complex, multifaceted lives, frequently prove not as easily manipulated by the biases and cognitive heuristics atop which the insights of behavioral economics rest. Controlled experiments yield controlled, and thereby limited, insights and the college students who participated in the experiments are different from the typical worker.

For scholars working in the fields of organizational behavior and human relations, missing was the sort of leg work visible in the scholarship of Tsedal Neeley, David Thomas, and John Gabarro, not to mention their academic progenitors, Donham, Henderson, Roethlisberger, and Mayo. Indeed, what was especially lauded about Banerjee's and Duflo's work in *Poor Economics*, was their willingness to closely observe the decision making of the globally poor. This feature of their work is laudable. What it isn't is revolutionary or rare. Rather, it reflects approaches and insights long established and decades-practiced by medical model adherents in the field of organizational behavior.

Conclusion

This book publishes at a troubling time. As I write, the world is slowly, awkwardly emerging from a pandemic and entering economic turbulence, political turbulence, and social and cultural turbulence. Our problems—local, national, and global—are real and solutions seem in short supply.

The business school was born in a moment of similar confusion. The world before and after World War II was a tumultuous world in need of improving solutions sought by the ethically responsible. The first business schools were invented with the transparent intent of finding these solutions. That among the four men at the center of HBS's origin story—Henderson, Roethlisberger, Mayo, and Donham—there was a graduate of the Harvard Medical School, and a trained psychologist is only partly why they coalesced around what I've termed the medical model of listen, observe, and test. Like physicians, they were focused on providing help, while doing no harm. Their patch was the business world, and the field they invented was organizational behavior, a systems-approach diagnostic method that understood real-time, real-world listening, observing, and testing were requisite.

Of grave concern is that today our own turbulent world lacks business schools producing scholars and scholarship similarly focused on methods of discovering and improving solutions. Instead, the 21st century meets its turmoil with a business school ecosystem under significant distress.

As we have seen, this crisis of business education and scholarship has been brewing for nearly three generations. During that time, we've lost talent. I've seen colleagues (including our new doctoral students) throw up their hands and walk away, taking jobs in other sectors where they feel they can make a difference. I know junior scholars who, under the publish-or-perish dictate, check boxes for advancement by solving narrow, academic problems. And I know editors who experience the publish-or-perish problem from the opposite end of the gun, caught between esoteric scholarship or solutionless-but-digestible business publishing "lite." I've seen a sense of paralysis and cynicism take hold.

I've also seen research that was once relevant and useful to the business community disappear, replaced by the studies of quants increasingly remote from the needs of the real world.

What is to be done? To echo the old adage, physician, heal thyself, I recommend in the spirit of this very book that those in charge of overseeing the world's business schools listen, observe, and test.

Within the walls of the academy, we must change our practices so that the spirit of exploration, which is integral to the process of scientific discovery, in the truest sense of that term, is again nurtured and fortified. Young people joining the field must be encouraged to develop research plans where the solutions they find can make a difference in the real world. Today, the psychic toll of the academic rat race is simply not worth it, given that the afflicted are toiling toward no meaningful end. Those of us raised in the human relations tradition had it so much easier. We worked no less hard than our quant successors, but our work was imbued with a shared sense of curiosity and adventure. We were not inherently more curious or creative than those entering the field today; on the contrary, we, too, were just kids who wanted jobs. But 60 years ago, the field was still relatively new and much was still unknown ("nascent"). We were invited to pursue our passion, knowing we would be rewarded: we could get those desirable jobs by finding a puzzle we couldn't let go of and, by seeking creative means to solve it, translate our questions into a research agenda that could improve real-world practice. Back then, young scholars were encouraged to build a coherent research plan that could be pursued for an entire career, with knowledge-building as the goal. Today, as one junior colleague pointed out, research agendas are a patchwork affair assembled on the basis of prior hits and shaped by the pursuit of further ones. It seems to me a crime to rob today's enthusiastic young people of their inquisitiveness and deny them the opportunity for adventure just because the academy demands X number of successful publications to achieve tenure. We need to do better than that.

As well, it used to be that the academic-appointments process was a holistic, local affair. Faculties and deans had independent definitions of quality; as a result, different schools prioritized different aspects of scholarship, and varying traditions flourished across the intellectual landscape.[1] At HBS, in service of our tradition of practitioner-oriented field research, appointments committees considered a candidate's teaching skill and potential for practical impact, giving credit for something more than scholarly publications. An approach like this isn't perfect, and it is essential that those with the audacity to restore it learn from past mistakes. Discretion can be misused, after all. It can also be used wisely, within parameters designed to mitigate prejudice.

The alternative we now rely on is much worse. Supposedly, hiring is now based on objective, quantifiable criteria of merit, but this notion is not to be believed. What has happened is that one, debatable sense of merit—that prized by quants, or those scholars and administrators who seek in statistics plausible deniability of subjectivity—has displaced all others. Instead of intellectually adventurous faculties with diverse points of view, business scholarship is a monoculture. Those institutions considered to be at the top of the heap hire from each other, fostering homogeneity. The preference for faculty with doctorates means that more and more instructors have no real-world experience when they enter academia; students are going straight from undergraduate study to doctoral study and then the faculty lounge. Even HBS looks a lot more like its peers these days, whereas at one time the faculty was a mix of academics and practice-oriented scholars who did not necessarily have PhDs and who worked in real organizations, whether as employees or consultants.

This shift in priorities within academia's walls would not entail innovation, but it would begin to answer the second challenge we face, what must be changed so that our work remains relevant to the world outside these walls. Business schools are supposed to serve business and society at large. We don't need new priorities; we need to realign with our own missions. The mission statements of most business schools echo the vision of social responsibility and practical impact put forth by Donham a century ago. HBS's stated purpose is to "educate leaders who make a difference in the world." That purpose, alas, guides only a minority of our faculty, and the proportion is even lower at most other business schools.

As Donham, Henderson, May, and Roethlisberger understood, along with the generations of scholars that followed immediately in their wake, the problems of the real world demand a different approach. They require a professional ethic of do no harm. And they accomplish the most good when they, in manner and methods echoing their professional peers, physicians, directly listen, observe, and test. A diagnosis of problems, managerial or medicinal, arrived at from the comfort of a laboratory of a faculty lounge are insufficient. We can, indeed we must, do better.

Our field was founded to address challenges arising from changing forms of work in light of new technology and growing economy; today, workers once again face unease from our era's innovations. Artificial intelligence and automation have already changed working life for many, and the effects will only be magnified in the years to come. Meanwhile, the gig economy has dramatically altered schedules, compensation arrangements, employee benefits, and the relationship between workers and the organizations that pay them. Business schools need to dedicate their resources of people, time, and money to supporting fieldwork to explore solutions to these and other real-world challenges.

For example, what are the consequences of today's human–machine interactions? Drivers for ride services like Uber and Lyft get work assignments from computers, limiting their contact with other human beings in their companies. At the same time, increasing numbers of employees in offices, factories, and warehouses do jobs that primarily involve monitoring the performance of electromechanical equipment. What happens to their relationships with co-workers, if indeed they have any? What happens to their relationship with their boss? Perhaps most importantly, how do these changes affect their motivation and job satisfaction? And vast areas of the economy remain little explored. Few researchers have spent much time on organizational behavior in agriculture or in the new firms sprouting up in the postindustrial Midwest, focused on high-tech manufacturing.

Those who still have jobs are the lucky ones who have not yet lost their work to machines. What about those who have in fact lost jobs to these new technologies and have not found new ones? And why are so many people leaving the work force and choosing not to return? This issue was exacerbated by the Covid-19 pandemic, but what has been called the Great Resignation predates that. HBS-style research, involving careful qualitative study, can help us better understand what working life is not providing people, so that they prefer to leave their jobs and find new ones, including nontraditional careers.

Another critical issue is income inequality. Understanding the causes and impact of the growing income gap is a job for economists, but there is a facet of this trend that is squarely within the purview of organizational scholars: the rapidly rising compensation of CEOs as compared to other senior executives and in the face of relatively static pay for all other employees. How are these massive reward discrepancies affecting subordinates, whether other executives or the larger base of employees? Are boards of directors monitoring these rewards and compensation?

A further issue facing American society is the struggle for social justice. Diversity remains fraught in corporate America, perhaps now even more so than 20 years ago. Competition for jobs is fierce and many challenges still exist for minorities trying to move up in their careers and for the managers and human resource specialists supporting them. This too is a topic that organizational behavior scholars, using field research methods, can illuminate. Indeed, some already have.

And there are many more issues to address. Not only do employees of global companies communicate in different languages, but they are also geographically dispersed in different time zones, and this too complicates the act of making joint decisions. What, from the standpoint of employees, is the best way to handle time zone differences? How can leaders build a sense of teamwork across international boundaries and time zones, and of course national culture? What sort of workers handle these circumstances well, and which don't? Are the youngest workers a good choice for global companies? They are known for openness to diverse perspectives, but at the same time change jobs frequently. Are they eager and curious about working with genuine strangers, or are the associated difficulties enough to push them out of a globally distributed organization? In short, the opportunities for research are abundant. Scholars in our field should seize them.

Consider the manifold benefits that would accrue to business scholarship publicly addressing these most-relevant, most-immediately experienced economic and social problems. Our research and findings wouldn't be relegated so exclusively to the "business book" sections of media and bookstores. Our scholars and students would enjoy a stature other than, perhaps even eclipsing, facilitators of consulting services lining the pockets of an elite few. Like physicians turned to in the moment of pandemics, business scholars could be turned to in moments of economic and industrial turbulence. Even when we don't have solutions, being understood as the branch of scholarship that is tasked with helping find them would be morale boosting for our faculty and students. What is more, given the global reach of business, such scholarship holds out promise to help address problems around the world.

I am under no illusions that it will be easy to reorient organizational scholarship. It's hard to tell the emperor that he has no clothes, or, more politely, that his clothes aren't the only outfit in town. It's hard to turn a battleship and stop a runaway train. But sometimes it's necessary. Happily, we have a framework to guide us. For nearly a century, we've known how to do problem-centered humanistic research that addresses social change and unrest. Assemble thinkers from different disciplines, à la Henderson and Mayo; review the existing literature; bring in truckloads of data gathered in the field; and apply clinical methods of listening, observation, testing, diagnosis, and treatment, oscillating between inductive findings, provisional hypotheses, and further testing. Train the next generation through cross-disciplinary seminars and curricula.

Born at a moment when the Industrial Revolution was truly a labor revolution, the human relations movement attacked the problems before it by wading into the zone of action. Our own era of disruption and upheaval, with real problems clamoring for attention and begging for solutions, echoes that earlier time. When a new disease appears on the horizon, a clinical approach that thoroughly investigates the phenomena is our best chance to find a treatment or cure. When territory is unfamiliar, a pioneering expedition will allow us to make our way through the wilderness.

Today, serious thinking about business should be about actual businesses, not ideal models. We must again wade into the action, bringing with us a keen sense of adventure and the strong motivation to address social problems. We must renew our understanding of business as a human project, comprising real people with complicated lives of which work is an important, but not the only, part. Rather than write off puzzling facts as inconsistent with theory, we must scrutinize those puzzling facts that much more closely.

Listen, observe, test—this is the method that restored humanity from the inhumane context of scientific management, that indelibly changed how workers and their supervisors relate to each other, that pressed organizations to confront the reality that the people working for them are not just cogs in machine—they are people! That method still works, and it will always work because it speaks to a very basic truth. Life does not sit us down in an armchair and reveal itself to us. Only when we go out into the world, meet its inhabitants, and give them the opportunity to tell their stories, do we even begin to understand what it means to work together. We must return to this method and use it to understand and cope with the very real challenges that we are facing once again.

Notes

Introduction

1. Lawrence (1992), p. 140.

Chapter 1

1. Roethlisberger (1939), p. 358.
2. Roethlisberger (1968), p. 153.
3. Roethlisberger (1968), p. 123.
4. Henderson (1926), p. 1.
5. "It has been said with much truth that scientific management is like the invention of machinery in its effect upon workers and social conditions and welfare generally—that it gives a new impulse to the industrial revolution which characterized the latter part of the eighteenth and nineteenth centuries and strengthens its general effects and tendencies." *The Commission on Industrial Relations Final Report* (1912), p. 142.
6. Taylor (1911), p. 7.
7. A book from 1948 about the Gilbreths, *Cheaper by the Dozen*, written by two of their offspring, F.B. Gilbreth Jr. and E.G. Carey, offers a comedic view of efficiency theory as applied to a household with 12 children, but in reality, this "scientific" approach gave factory workers little to smile about.
8. Henderson (1927), pp. 61–62.
9. Laboratory correspondence. October 22, 1934. Lawrence Joseph Henderson papers, Carton 3, Folder 52, HBS Archives, Baker Library, Harvard Business School. An article by G. Edgar Folk. 2010. "The Harvard Fatigue Laboratory: contributions to World War II," *Advances in Physiology Education* 34, no. 3 records though the following reminiscence: "Although humans were the subjects of

most Fatigue Laboratory studies while I was there, I found when I looked at the past publications from the Fatigue Laboratory that there were reprints concerned with comparative physiology. The system seemed to work this way: although the goal was always to obtain knowledge on human physiology, the techniques were also used on some convenient vertebrate to record their physiology. For example, someone had brought two crocodiles into the laboratory, and their blood was analyzed with the same techniques as ordinarily applied to human subjects."

10. Hounshell (1985), pp. 220–224, 228. For an excellent account of the types of machinery that made up the assembly line, see the same work. The price of the 1904 Model B's comes from Kimes (1996).
11. Hounshell (1985), p. 247.
12. Sward (1948), p. 47.
13. Acc. 1, Fair Lane Paper, IV. Ford Motor Company, "Personal Complaints" Box 120. Ford Archives.
14. Hounshell (1985), p. 259.
15. Industrial Accident Statistics, Bul, Whole No. 157, U.S. Bureau of Labor Statistics (1915).
16. Troy (1965), p. 93.
17. American Manufacturer and Iron World (1901).
18. Ingham (1991), p. 356 writes, "From a manager's point of view the pooling system was ideal: it made each man and each group of men their own monitors in keeping up speed and disciplines. But the men were often forced to work at a feverish pace; they were responsible for mistakes made either by another gang, or by company foremen, which reduced their weekly earnings…It was this rigorous but logical extension of the ideas of scientific management which led directly to the McKees Rocks strike of 1909."
19. National Labor Tribune (1909).
20. "The company has not agreed or promised to increase at this time the wages of its workmen, but does expect that as general business conditions improve its workmen will share the benefits…the company has not promised to abandon the pooling system…the company will not tolerate any graft." Independent, September 16, 1909.
21. Edwin Gay quoted by Cruikshank (1987), p. 44.

22. Ibid.
23. Donham (1927), p. 406.
24. Ibid, p. 409.
25. Ibid, p. 406.
26. Donham (1927), p. 401.
27. Donham (1943), p. 46.
28. Henderson (1927). A speech delivered at the spring meeting of the American Association of the Collegiate Schools of Business.
29. Indeed, until the late 1920s, Henderson's primary authority on the observation of human behavior was the French satirical playwright Molière, from whom he learned "most about what good observation is and how it is possible to generalize from the complex reality of everyday life." Henderson (1936), p. 35.
30. Smith (1986), p. 51.
31. Russet (1966), p. 112. Henderson was so convinced of the importance of systems that he compared them to a law of nature, writing that "just as Newton first conclusively showed that this is a world of masses, so Willard Gibbs first revealed it as a world of systems." He also explained the kind of analysis necessary to understand systems: It was his fundamental belief that "in organic processes, cause-and-effect analysis leads, in general, to erroneous conclusions. The only alternative…is mutual dependence analysis," a conviction which later drew him to Pareto.
32. Because Wheeler's specialty was the social behavior of insects, he was interested in the social behavior of other species, including human beings. When Harvard awarded Wheeler an honorary degree, President Lowell composed the citation himself: "he has shown that insects, like men, can construct societies without the use of reason." Roethlisberger (1977), p. 61.
33. Roethlisberger (1977), p. 61.
34. For example, Pareto's most famous economic theory, known as the Pareto principle or the 80/20 rule, grew from his observation that eighty percent of Italy's land was owned by twenty percent of the population. Benoit Mandelbrot describes the inductive research that led to Pareto's rule, including tax records from Basel, Switzerland, dating from 1454, and from Augsburg, Germany, in 1471, 1498

and 1512. He also researched rental income from Paris and personal income from Britain, Prussia, Saxony, Ireland, Italy, and Peru. When he plotted income on one axis, and number of people with that income on the other, the same picture kept emerging, regardless of location or era. The data did not fall into a bell curve, as would be expected in a random distribution of wealth; it was "an arrow," wide at the bottom (the mass of men) and narrow at the top (the wealthy elite). Pareto's conclusion: his rule was '…a social law, something in the nature of man.' Mandelbrot (2006), p. 153.

35. Pareto (1917).

36. Riccioni (2021), p. 306.

37. Cabot and Kahl (1956), p. 34.

38. Henderson (1975), p. 284.

39. Roethlisberger (1977), pp. 67–68.

40. Roethlisberger (1968), p. 263.

41. Trahair (2017), p. 116.

42. Ibid, p. 190.

43. Ibid, p. 172. The words are Trahair's, the sentiment Mayo's.

44. Ibid, p. 257.

45. Roethlisberger (1977), p. 50.

46. Trahair (2017), p. 202.

47. Roethlisberger (1977), p. 32.

48. Roethlisberger (1947), p. 160. "In our journey through the field of social science…we encountered one class of social scientists from whom we received little or no assistance. We shall give this class no title, for its members are legion and bear many different labels. Some have 'chairs' in academic institutions; some do not. They all, however, have certain characteristics in common. Unlike the inarticulate men of action, they are people who are very articulate in discussing matters with which they sometimes have little first-hand acquaintance or experience. Some of them are 'teachers,' but they do not practice any skills, other than verbal ones, relating to social phenomena."

49. Malinowski (2005 [1922]), p. 19.

50. Trahair and Zelenik (2017), p. 84.

51. Radcliffe-Brown (1935), p. 394.

52. Ibid.

53. These associated included, Osgood Lovekin, one of Mayo's MBA students, and Emily Osborne. A nurse and researcher at the University of Pennsylvania Medical School, who assisted with the Philadelphia textile-workers study, Osborne became Mayo's long-time secretary and research assistant at Harvard.

54. Donham (1937), p. 105.

55. Letter from E. Mayo to W. Donham, Elton Mayo Papers, Series II HBS Materials 1925-1947, Subseries A HBS General Materials, Harvard Business School Archives, Baker Library, Harvard Business School, p. 3.

56. Ibid.

57. Letter from E. Mayo to W. Donham, September 1928. Elton Mayo Papers, Series II HBS Materials 1925-1947, Subseries A HBS General Materials, Harvard Business School Archives, Baker Library, Harvard Business School.

58. Gillespie (1993), p. 119.

59. Trahair and Zelenik (2017), p. 84.

60. Letter from E. Mayo to Colonel A. Woods, November 20, 1928. Elton Mayo Papers, Series I Correspondence 1913-1960, Subseries B. Professional Correspondence, 1992-1947, Harvard Business School Archives, Baker Library, Harvard Business School, p. 4.

61. Roethlisberger (1977), p. 22.

62. Ibid, p. 21.

63. Ibid, p. 25.

64. Ibid, p. 26.

65. Ibid, p. 27: "When I told him of my plight, I expected he would be as horrified as I and that he would banish me to Dantes' ninth circuit of purgatory. Instead, he seemed curious and amused. His amusement bothered me a little, but when he offered me a job it put a different complexion on the matter. If he could resurrect the unholy and the damned for something useful then I was all for him."

66. Ibid, p. 60.

67. Huxley (1893–1894) 'Biogenesis and Abiogenesis,' in *Collected Essays.*

Chapter 2

1. Gillespie (1991/1993), p. 14.
2. Charles Dubois (Western Electric president), quoted in Dietz (1925), p. 105. Analysts of the Hawthorne studies have noted that the apparent progressivism of Western Electric masks paternalism and anti-union bias. See Hassard (2012), pp. 1431–1461. The discouragement of unions is also mentioned in the Harvard Business School Baker Library archival report on the Hawthorne studies. www.library.hbs.edu/hc/hawthorne/02.html (September 2022).
3. Hall (1922), p. 8.
4. Ibid, p. 4.
5. Gillespie (1991/1993), pp. 39–40.
6. Dickinson and Roethlisberger (1939, reprinted 2003), p. 577.
7. Ibid, p. 591.
8. Ibid, pp. 578–579, 591–592.
9. Gillespie (1991/1993), p. 119.
10. Domhoff. (1990), p. 77.
11. Gillespie (1991/1993), p. 119.
12. Ibid, pp. 41–42.
13. Gillespie (1991/1993), p. 43. See Appendix H, "Factory Illumination--Production Tests at Hawthorne Works of the Western Electric Co.," p. 8.
14. Dickinson and Roethlisberger (1939, reprinted 2003), p. 19.
15. Ibid, pp. 28–29.
16. Ibid, p. 86.
17. Letter from E. Mayo to G. Pennock, September 8, 1928. Elton Mayo Papers, Series II HBS Materials 1925-1947, Subseries A HBS General Materials, Harvard Business School Archives, Baker Library, Harvard Business School.
18. This hypothesis generation "dictated the direction of the inquiry for many months to come." Dickinson and Roethlisberger (1939, reprinted 2003), p. 89.
19. Ibid, Chapter 5.
20. Ibid, Chapter 6.
21. Ibid, p. 160: "The efficacy of a wage incentive was so dependent on its relation to other factors that it was impossible to consider

it as a thing in itself having an independent effect on the individual. Only in connection with the interpersonal relations at work and the personal situations outside of work, to mention two important variables, could its effect on output be determined."

22. Ibid, p. 183.

23. Mayo (2004), p. 73.

24. Ibid.

25. Roethlisberger (1977), p. 47.

26. Ibid; Roethlisberger and Dickinson (1966) came out long after Management and the Worker (1939) and made use of some of the archived transcripts from the interviewing program at Hawthorne. The 1966 book may have been written partly to please Western Electric executives, and partly in the hope (grown somewhat faint) that Roethlisberger still had of integrating organizational structure and individual lives by teaching managers how to bridge the divide.

27. Dickinson and Roethlisberger (1939, reprinted 2003), pp. 202–203.

28. Mayo (2004), p. 92.

29. Gillespie (1991/1993), p. 134.

30. Mayo (1949), p. 23.

31. Dickinson and Roethlisberger (1939, reprinted 2003), p. 203.

32. Ibid, Chapter XIV, pp. 293–298, 301–307, 307–310.

33. Mayo (1930), pp. 326–332.

34. "Interview with Operator No. 2 from Relay Assembly Test Room, 1927–1932." (Western Electric Company Hawthorne Studies Collection, box 3C, folder 22)—(p. 197) Harvard Business School, Selected Digital Resources. https://iiif.lib.harvard.edu/manifests/view/drs:726549 7$1i (accessed January 2022).

35. Ibid.

36. Ibid.

37. Dickinson and Roethlisberger (1939, reprinted 2003), p. 324. I would add that gender may have played some role in the Relay Test Assembly Room, not noted at the time by the Hawthorne investigators. The cooperative spirit in the room and the high productivity despite many changes in the test room conditions possibly reflect the more collaborative approach to work typical of women. In contrast, in the Bank Wiring Observation Room, where all the workers were

men, informal social networks revealed competitive and aggressive "sentiments" and fluctuations in output associated with social control within a "masculine" hierarchy.

38. Ibid, p. 252.

39. Ibid, p. 376.

40. Ibid, p. 385: "In the interview situation the investigators obtained only statements of how the employees said they acted. The interviewers had no means of relating these statements to what actually transpired. This distinction between actions and words, or between overt and verbal behavior, is emphasized here because it led to an innovation in method which distinguished the study to be reported from all the others dealt with so far, namely, supplementing the interviewing method with direct observation."

41. Ibid, p. 522.

42. Ibid, pp. 413–414, 417–423.

43. Ibid, p. 522.

44. Roethlisberger (1977), p. 48; Dickinson and Roethlisberger (1939, reprinted 2003), p. 524.

45. Dickinson and Roethlisberger (1939, reprinted 2003), pp. 496–498, 507–510, 528.

46. Ibid, pp. 460–61, 470, 475.

47. Ibid, pp. 218.

48. Ibid, pp. 328.

49. Roethlisberger (1951), p. 55.

50. Ibid.

51. Cabot (1942), p. 55.

52. Ibid, p. 160.

53. Roethlisberger (1977), pp. 52–53.

54. Dickinson and Roethlisberger (1939, reprinted 2003), p. 4.

55. Roethlisberger (1962), reprinted in Roethlisberger (1968), p. 280.

56. Gillespie (1991/1993), p. 256

57. Roethlisberger (1977), p. 106.

58. MBA Course Catalog, Vol. XLIX, No. 12 (May 26, 1952), p. 48; Humans Relations was led by Roethlisberger from 1948-1952, by George Lombard from 1952–1962, and then by Art Turner.

59. Roethlisberger (1977), p. 198.

60. Homans (1941), p. 402.

61. Roethlisberger (1977), p. 238.

62. Zaleznik, Homans, and Roethlisberger (1958), p. 389.

Chapter 3

1. Master's Series on Field Research—Interview with Professor George Lombard (2021).

2. Lawrence, Barnes and Lorsch (1976), p. 3.

3. Lawrence, Barnes and Lorsch (1976), p. 4.

4. Lawrence and Turner (1965), p. 15.

5. Spencer (1904), pp. 55–56.

6. In the course of my research, I found that what others had called heterogeneity was also labeled differentiation, and that differentiation and integration were considered opposite forces. This inherent conflict became one of my central ideas for understanding the problems of structuring and leading larger organizations–what Paul and I, and eventually our colleagues, began calling "D and I," "Differentiation and Integration." See for example, Ronken and Lawrence (1952).

7. Lawrence and Lorsch (1967), p. 142.

8. See for example, among many others, Gilson (1940), pp. 98–101; Bell (1947), pp. 79–88; Dunlop (1950), pp. 383–393.

9. Lawrence and Lorsch (1967), p. 143.

10. Ibid, p. 103.

11. Ibid, p. 138.

12. Ibid, pp. 156–158.

13. Donaldson (2001), p. 4.

Chapter 4

1. Walton (1972), pp. 70–81.

2. Personal interview with R.E. Walton (November 2018).

3. Ibid.

4. Walton (1975), p. 140.

5. Personal interview with R.E. Walton (November 2018).

6. Walton (1972), p. 71.

7. Walton (1975), p. 140.

8. Walton (1975), p. 147.

9. Personal interview with R.E. Walton (November 2018).

10. Walton (1975), p. 149.

11. Ibid, p. 142.

12. Ibid, p. 143.

13. Walton (1975), p. 145.

14. Study by R. Schrank, found in Walton (1975), p. 145.

15. Walton (1977), p. 154.

16. Personal interview with R.E. Walton (November 2018).

17. Ibid.

18. Kotter and Lawrence (1974).

19. Kotter (1982), p. 2.

20. Ibid, p. 156.

21. Ibid, p. 130. The authors of In Search of Excellence, published the same year, made much the same point and, indeed, owe a debt to the work of scholars like Kotter, who supplied data supporting their position.

22. Ibid, p. 3.

23. Ibid, p. 8.

24. Personal Conversation with J. Kotter (November 2019).

25. Gabarro (1987), p. 6.

26. Ibid, p. 8.

27. Ibid, p. 68.

28. Of John Kotter she says, "I now realize I must have frustrated him to death, because the only way I knew how to think about doing the study was statistically, so I was trying to make him design it to be rigorous from a statistical point of view—you know, these surveys and things. But that really wasn't how he was thinking about it." Personal conversation with Linda Hill (November 2019).

29. Hill cites Sayles (1989); Kotter (1982); Stewart (1982); Mintzberg (1973).

30. Hill (2019), p. 305.

31. Ibid, p. 338.

32. Ibid, p. 307.

33. Ibid, p. 305.
34. Ibid, p. 307.
35. Ibid, p. 322.
36. Ibid, p. 15.
37. Ibid, p. 209.
38. Ibid, p. 275.
39. Snook, Nohria, and Khurnana (2011), p. 104.
40. Personal interview with L. Hill (November 2019).
41. Hill (2019), p. xii.
42. Hill's interest in the topic ultimately led to her founding of the Leadership Initiative at HBS.
43. Hill and Lineback (2011), p. xii.
44. Lorsch and Tierney (2002), p. 4.
45. Ibid, pp. 8–9.

Chapter 5

1. Martin and Lorsch (1992), pp. 59–77.
2. Gabarro and Thomas (1999).
3. David and Gabarro (n.d.), p. 11.
4. Neeley (2019).
5. Ibid, p. 4.
6. Roethlisberger (1963), p. 182.
7. Roethlisberger (1968), p. viii.
8. Ibid, pp. x–xi.
9. Roethlisberger (1977), p. 322.
10. Bell (1947), p. 88.
11. McNair (1957), p. 30.
12. Ibid, p. 20.
13. See for example O'Reilly and Tushman (2007), p. 770. I'll note here that when it comes to relevance, it's not either/or. Theoretical abstraction and remoteness from the phenomena are intimately intertwined.
14. Ozcelik and Barsade (2018), pp. 2343–2366.
15. Using a "mediator–moderator" analysis, a favored approach in scholarly business journals, the authors differentiate between causal elements and those that merely influence the strength of a correlation.

They quantify all elements: The self-report of workers on their loneliness and on their affective commitment to the organization (mediators) and employee approachability (as rated by co-workers) and work group cultures characterized by either companionate love or anger (moderators).

16. Ozcelik and Barsade (2018), pp. 2343–2366, acknowledge the problem: "…we cannot confirm causality. There is a possibility, for example, that poorer performance leads employees to be isolated from their co-workers, leading to greater loneliness…" p. 2361.

17. Ozcelik and Barsade (2018), p. 2361, 2354; J. Pearl discusses the problem of "overcontrolling," including for variables that may, in fact, be causal (n.d.) pp. 138–139.

18. Yu, Matta, and Cornfield (2018), pp. 1158–1188.

19. Jensen and Meckling (1976), pp. 305–360.

20. Ibid (1976), p. 312.

21. Anonymous.

22. Yu, Matta, and Cornfield (2018), p. 1169.

23. As a point of contrast: in the Prediction Study from some seventy years ago, Roethlisberger puzzled over the lack of correlation between "distributive justice" and worker satisfaction, until he consulted the "soft, gooey data" of interviews that revealed differences in psychological temperament and history. See Roethlisberger (1977), p. 238.

24. Theeke, Polidoro, and Fredrickson (2013), p. 910.

25. Shi, Connelly, and Cirik (2018), pp. 1892–1919.

26. Hambrick (1994), p. 13. Hambrick delivered the speech at Columbia University. He holds an MBA from HBS and a PhD from Penn State University, where he is currently Smeal Professor of Management; he is also Bronfman Professor Emeritus at Columbia.

27. Ibid.

28. Anonymous.

29. Martin (2012), pp. 293–299.

30. Various private conversations with younger colleagues. The relevance of this sort of research has been a growing concern over the last decade or so. See for example, Lambert (2019), pp. 382–394; Fox and Groesser (2016), pp. 457–465.

31. As my colleague Rakesh Khurana and his co-author Spender (2012), p. 636 posed the issue: "What are we preparing our students for—to be able to compete in publications and scholarly recognition with students trained in traditional disciplinary settings, albeit while working in a business school setting? Or do we hope to train 'first-class' students with a genuine curiosity towards the complexities of the executive process at the intersection of discipline-based knowledge and business practice?"

32. Glick, Miller, and Cardinal (2007), p. 830.

33. Edmonson and McManus (2007), pp. 1155–1179.

34. Petriglieri, Ashford, and Wreszniewski (2019), pp. 124–170; Valentine (2018), pp. 2081–2105; Debenigno (2017), pp. 526–569; Lifshitz-Assaf (2018), pp. 746–782.

35. The editors' reservations regarding the researcher's experience and role, expressed in the AMJ editorial on qualitative research relates to a lingering question about the "Hawthorne effect" and critics' charge of subjective bias in the original studies. See Bansal, Smith, and Vaara (2018), pp. 1189–1196.

Conclusion

1. Such variation made it more difficult to transfer accomplishments from one institution to another (what was considered worthy of promotion at Michigan might carry little value at Chicago, and vice versa), but also allowed different research paradigms to coexist.

References

American Manufacturer and Iron World. January 31, 1901. Pittsburgh: National Iron and Steel Pub. Co.

Bansal, P., W.K. Smith, and E. Vaara. August 2018. "New Ways of Seeing Through Qualitative Research." *Academy of Management Journal* 61, no. 4, pp. 1189–1196.

Bell, D. 1947. "Adjust Men to Machines." *Commentary* 3, pp. 79–88.

Bell, D. 1947. "Adjusting Men to Machines" *Commentary* 4, p. 88.

Cabot, H. and J.A. Kahl. 1956. *Human Relations: Concepts and Cases in Concrete Social Science*, p. 34. Cambridge, MA: Harvard University Press.

Cabot, P. 1942. *Addresses 1935–1941*, p. 55, 160. Cambridge, MA: Riverside Press.

Cruikshank, J.L. 1987. *A Delicate Experiment: The Harvard Business School, 1908–1945*, p. 44. Boston, MA: Harvard Business School Press.

David, T. and J. Gabarro. *Breaking Through: How People of Color—and the Companies They Work for—Can Overcome Barriers*, p. 11. Boston, MA: Harvard Business School Press.

Debenigno, J. June 2017. "Anchored Personalization in Managing Goal Conflict Between Professional Groups: The Case of U.S. Army Mental Health Care." *Administrative Science Quarterly* 63, no. 3, pp. 526–569.

Dickinson, W. and F. Roethlisberger. 1939, reprinted 2003. "Dictated the Direction of the Inquiry for Many Months to Come." *Management and the Worker*, p. 89. New York, NY and London: Routledge Press.

Dickinson, W. and F.J. Roethlisberger. 1939, reprinted 2003. *Management and the Worker*, pp. 4–592. New York, NY and London: Routledge Press.

Dickinson, W. and F. Roethlisberger. 1939, reprinted 2003. *Management and the Worker*, Chapters XIV, 5, and 6. New York, NY and London: Routledge Press.

Dietz, J.W. May 1925. "Some Aspects of Personnel Research in a Manufacturing Organization." *Annals of the American Academy of Political and Social Science* 119, no. 1, p. 105.

Domhoff, G.W. 1990. *The Power Elite and the State: How Policy Is Made in America*, p. 77. New York, NY and London: Routledge.

Donaldson, L. 2001. *The Contingency Theory of Organizations*, p. 4. Newbury Park, CA: Sage Publishing.

Donham, W.B. July 1927. "The Emerging Profession of Business." *Harvard Business Review* 5, p. 401, 406–409.

Donham, W.B. 1937. "The Importance of Research in Human Biology in a Faculty of Business Administration." Transcript of discussion in *Conference on a Scientific Study of Industrial Labor Conditions*, p. 105. Washington, D.C.: National Research Council.

Donham, W.B. 1943. "Biographical Memorial for L.J. Henderson." *National Academy of Sciences* 23, p. 46.

Dunlop, J.T. 1950. "Framework for the Analysis of Industrial Relations: Two Views." *Industrial and Labor Relations Review*, 3, pp. 383–393.

Edmonson, A. and S. McManus. 2007. "Methodological Fit in Management Field Research." *Academy of Management Review* 32, no. 4, pp. 1155–1179.

Fox, S. and S.N. Groesser. October 2016. "Reframing the Relevance of Research to Practice." *European Management Journal* 34, no. 5, pp. 457–465.

Gabarro, J. 1987. *The Dynamics of Taking Charge*, pp. 6–68. Boston, MA: Harvard Business Press.

Gabarro, J. and D. Thomas. 1999. *Breaking Through: The Making of Minority Executives in Corporate America*. Boston, MA: Harvard Business Review Press.

Gillespie, R. 1991/1993. *Manufacturing Knowledge—A History of the Hawthorne Experiments*, no. 5, pp. 14–256. Cambridge: Cambridge University Press.

Gilson, M. 1940. "Management and the Worker." *American Journal of Sociology* 46, pp. 98–101.

Glick, W.H., C.C. Miller, and L.B. Cardinal. 2007. "Making a Life in the Field of Organization Science." *Journal of Organizational Behavior* 28, no. 7, p. 830.

Hall, E.K. November 9, 1922. "Management's Responsibility for and Opportunities in the Personnel Job." *American Management Association, Convention Address Series*, pp. 4–8.

Hambrick, D.C. 1994. "What If the Academy Actually Mattered?" *The Academy of Management Review* 19, no. 1, p. 13.

Hassard, J.S. 2012. "Rethinking the Hawthorne Studies: The Western Electric Research in its Social, Political and Historical Context." *Human Relations* 65, no. 11, pp. 1431–1461.

Henderson, L.J. December 12, 1926. "Untitled and Unpublished Paper." *Henderson Papers*, p. 1. Baker Library Archives.

Henderson, L.J. December 1927. "Business Education as Envisaged by the Scientist." *HBSAB* 4, no. 2, pp. 61–62.

Henderson, L.J. September 21, 1936. "Memories." *LJHP*, unpublished manuscript, box 7, p. 35.

Henderson, L.J. 1975. "Hippocrates and the Practice of Medicine." In *The Practical Cogitator*, eds. C.P. Curtis, p. 284. New York, NY: Dell Publishing Co.

Hill, L.A. 2019. *Becoming a Manager*, pp. xii–338. Boston, MA: Harvard Business Review Press.

Hill, L. and K. Lineback. 2011. *Being the Boss*, p. xii. Boston, MA: Harvard Business Review Press.

Homans, G. 1941. *English Villages of the Thirteenth Century*, p. 402. Cambridge, MA: Harvard University Press.

Hounshell, D. 1985. *From the American System to Mass Production, 1800–1932: The Development of Manufacturing Technology in the United States*, pp. 220–259. Baltimore, MD: Johns Hopkins University Press.

Independent. September 16, 1909.

Ingham, J.N. 1991. *Making Iron and Steel: Independent Mills in Pittsburgh 1820–1929*, p. 356. Columbus Ohio: Ohio State University Press

Jensen, M.C. and W.H. Meckling. 1976. "Theory of the Firm: Managerial Behavior, Agency Costs and Ownership Structure." *Journal of Financial Economics* 3, no. 4, pp. 305–360.

Khurana, R. and J.C. Spender. 2012. "Herbert A Simon on What Ails Business Schools: More Than 'A Problem in Organization Design." *Journal of Management Studies* 49, no. 3, p. 636.

Kimes, B. 1996. *Standard catalog of American Cars 1805–1942*. Stevens Point, WI: Krause Publications.

Kotter, J. 1982. *The General Managers*, pp. 2–156. New York, NY: Free Press.

Kotter, J. 2008. *A Force for Change*, pp. 3–8. New York, NY: Simon and Schuster.

Kotter, J. and P. Lawrence. 1974. *Mayors in Action: Five Approaches to Urban Governance*. Hoboken, NJ: John Wiley & Sons, Inc.

Lambert, D.M. 2019. "Rediscovering Relevance." *The International Journal of Logistics Management* 30, no. 2, pp. 382–394.

Lawrence, P. June 1992. "The Challenge of Problem-Oriented Research." *Journal of Management Inquiry*, p. 140.

Lawrence, P. and J. Lorsch. 1967. *Organization and Environment*, pp. 103–158, Tables IV-6 and Table VI-I. Boston, MA: Harvard Business School Press.

Lawrence, P. and J. Lorsch. November–December 1967. "New Management Job, The Integrator." *Harvard Business Review*, 45, no. 6, pp. 142–143.

Lawrence, P. and A. Turner. 1965. *Industrial Jobs and the Workers an Investigation of Response to Task Attributes*, p. 15. Boston, MA: Harvard University Graduate School of Business Administration.

Lawrence, P., L.B. Barnes, and J. Lorsch. 1976. *Organizational Behavior and Administration: Cases and Readings*, pp. 3–4. Homewood, IL: Richard D. Irwin, Inc.

Lifshitz-Assaf, H. December 2018. "Dismantling Knowledge Boundaries at NASA: The Critical Role of Professional Identity in Open Innovation." *Administrative Science Quarterly* 63, no. 4, pp. 746–782.

Lorsch, J. and T. Tierney. 2002. *Aligning the Stars*, pp. 4–9. Boston, MA: Harvard Business Review Press.

Malinowski, B. 2005 [1922]. *Argonauts of the Western Pacific: An Account of Native Enterprise and Adventure in the Archipelagos of Melanesian New Guinea*, p. 19. London: Taylor & Francis.

Mandelbrot, B. 2006. "The Mystery of Cotton." *The Misbehavior of Markets: A Fractal View of Financial Turbulence*, p. 153. New York, NY: Basic Books.

Martin, R. March 2012. "The Cost of Actionability." *Academy of Management Learning and Education* 11, no. 2, pp. 293–299.

Martin, L. and J. Lorsch. November 1992. "A Modest Proposal for Improved Corporate Governance." *The Business Lawyer* 48, no. 1, pp. 59–77.

Mayo, E. 1930. "Changing Methods in Industry." *Personnel Journal* 8, pp. 326–332.

Mayo, E. 1949. *Some Notes on the Psychology of Pierre Janet*, p. 23. Cambridge, MA: Harvard University Press.

Mayo, E. 2004. *The Human Problems of an Industrial Civilization*, pp. 73–92. New York, NY and London: Routledge

McNair, M.P. March/April 1957. "Thinking Ahead: What Price Human Relations?" *Harvard Business Review* 35, no. 2, p. 30.

Mintzberg, H. 1973. *The Nature of Managerial Work*. New York, NY: Harper and Row.

National Labor Tribune. August 26, 1909.

Neeley, T. 2019. *The Language of Global Success*, p. 4. Princeton, NJ: Princeton University Press.

O'Reilly, C. and M. Tushman. 2007. "Dynamic Capabilities at IBM: Driving Strategy Into Action." *California Management Review* 49, no. 4, p. 770.

Ozcelik, H. and S.G. Barsade. 2018. "No Employee an Island: Workplace loneliness and Job Performance." *Academy of Management Journal* 61, no. 6, pp. 2343–2366.

Pareto, V. 1917. *Jubilee Speech at Lausanne*.

Pearl, J. n.d. *The Book of Why: The New Science of Cause and Effect*, pp. 138–39. New York, NY: Basic Books.

Petriglieri, G., S.J. Ashford, and A. Wreszniewski. 2019. "Agony and Ecstasy in the Gig Economy: Cultivating Holding Environments for Precarious and Personalized Work Identities." *Administrative Science Quarterly* 64, no. 1, pp. 124–170.

Radcliffe-Brown, A.R. 1935. "On the Concept of Function in Social Science." *American Anthropologist* 37, no. 3.1, p. 394.

Riccioni, I. 2021. "The Reality of Facts in the Sociology of Vilfredo Pareto: Remarks on Fiorenzo Mornati's biography of Vilfredo Pareto." *Revue Européenne des Sciences Sociales* 59, no. 2, p. 306.

Roethlisberger, F.J. October 1, 1977. *Elusive Phenomena: An Autobiographical Account of My Work in the Field of Organizational Behavior at the Harvard Business School*, p. 61. Boston, MA: Harvard Business School Press.

Roethlisberger, F. 1977. *Elusive Phenomena*, pp. 48–322. Cambridge, MA: Harvard University Press.

Roethlisberger, F.J. 1939. *Management and the Worker*, p. 358. Cambridge, MA: Harvard University Press.

Roethlisberger, F.J. 1947. *Management and Morale*, p. 160. Cambridge, MA: Harvard University Press.

Roethlisberger, F.J. 1951. "Training Supervisors in Human Relation." *The Case Method of Teaching Human Relations and Administration*, p. 55. Cambridge, MA: Harvard University Press.

Roethlisberger, F.J. 1962. "The Contributions of the Behavioral Sciences to a General Theory of Management." reprinted in Roethlisberger, F.J. 1968. *Man-in-Organization*, p. 280. Cambridge, MA: Harvard University Press.

Roethlisberger, F.J. 1968. "The Contributions of the Behavioral Sciences to a General Theory of Management." *Man-in-Organization*, p. 263. Cambridge, MA: Harvard University Press.

Roethlisberger, F.J. 1968. "The Human Equation in Employee Productivity." *Man-in-Organization*, pp. 123–153. Cambridge, MA: Harvard University Press.

Roethlisberger, F.J. 1968. *Man-in-Organization: Essays of F. J. Roethlisberger*, pp. viii–xi, 153. Cambridge, MA: Harvard University Press.

Roethlisberger, F.J. 1977. *Elusive Phenomena: An Autobiographical Account of My Work in the Field of Organizational Behavior at the Harvard Business School*, pp. 21–68. Boston, MA: Harvard Business School Press.

Roethlisberger, F.J. 1977. *Elusive Phenomena*, pp. 106–238. Cambridge, MA: Harvard University Press.

Roethlisberger, F.J. and W. Dickinson. 1966. *Counseling in an Organization*. Boston, MA.

Roethlisberger, F.J. Summer 1963. "The Territory and Skill of the Administrator." *Management of Personnel Quarterly* 2, no. 2, p. 182.

Ronken, H. and P. Lawrence. 1952. *Administering Changes: A Case Study of Human Relations in a Factory*. Boston, MA: Harvard Business School Division of Research.

Russet, C.E. 1966. *The Concept of Equilibrium in American. Social Thought*, p. 112. New Haven, CT and London: Yale University Press.

Roethlisberger, F. 1977. *Elusive Phenomena*, p. 238. Cambridge, MA: Harvard University Press.

Sayles, L.R. 1989. *Leadership in Real Organizations*. New York, NY: McGraw Hill.

Shi, W., B.L. Connelly, and K. Cirik. 2018. "Short Seller Influence on Firm Growth: A Threat Rigidity Perspective." *Academy of Management Journal* 61, no. 5, pp. 1892–1919.

Smith, R. 1986. *The American Business System and the Theory and Practice of Social Science: The Case of the Harvard Business School, 1925–1945*, p. 51. New York, NY: Garland Publishing.

Snook, S., N. Nohria, and R. Khurnana. 2011. *The Handbook for Teaching Leadership: Knowing, Doing and Being*, p. 104. Newbury Park, CA: Sage Publications.

Spencer, H. 1904. *An Autobiography: Herbert Spencer* 2, pp. 55–56. New York, NY: D. Appleton.

Stewart, R. 1982. *Choices for the Manager*. New York, NY: Prentice and Hall.

Sward, K. 1948. *The Legend of Henry Ford*, p. 47. New York, NY: Rhinehart Publishing.

Taylor, F.W. 1911. *Principles of Scientific Management*, p. 7. New York, NY and London: Harper Brothers.

The Commission on Industrial Relations Final Report. 1912. p. 142.

Theeke, M., F. Polidoro, Jr., and J.W. Fredrickson. December 2013. "Path-Dependent Routines in the Evaluations of Novelty: The Effects of Innovators' New Knowledge Use on Brokerage Firms' Coverage." *Administrative Science Quarterly* 58, no. 4, p. 910.

Trahair, R. 2017. *Elton Mayo: The Humanist Temper*, p. 116–257. London and New York, NY: Routledge.

Trahair, R. and A. Zeleznik. 2017. *Elton Mayo: The Humanist Temper*, p. 84. London and New York, NY: Routledge.

Troy, L. February 1965. "Trade Union Membership, 1897–1962." *The Review of Economics and Statistics* 47, no. 2, p. 93.

Valentine, M. 2018. "When Equity Seems Unfair: The Role of Justice Enforceablity in Temporary Team Coordination." *Academy of Management Journal* 61, no. 6, pp. 2081–2105.

Walton, R.E. 1975. "Using Social Psychology to Create a New Plant Culture." *Applying Social Psychology*, eds. M. Deutsch and H. Hornstein, pp. 140–149. New York, NY and London: Routledge.

Walton, R.E. 1977. "Work Innovations at Topeka: After Six Years." *The Journal of Applied Behavioral Science* 13, no. 3, p. 154.

Walton, R.E. November–December 1972. "How to Counter Alienation in the Plant." *Harvard Business Review* 72, no. 6, pp. 70–81.

Yu, A., F.K. Matta, and B. Cornfield. 2018. "Is Leader–Member Exchange Differentiation Beneficial or Detrimental for Group Effectiveness? A Meta-Analytic Investigation and Theoretical Integration." *Academy of Management Journal* 61, no. 3, pp. 1158–1188.

Zaleznik, A., C.R. Christensen, G. Homans, and F.J. Roethlisberger. 1958. *The Motivation, Satisfaction, and Productivity of Workers*, p. 389. Boston, MA: Division of Research Harvard Graduate School of Business.

Further Reading List

Christensen, C., D. Garvin, and A. Sweet. 1991. *Education for Judgment: The Artistry of Discussion Leadership*. Boston MA: Harvard Business School Press.

Homans, G.C. 1991. *The Human Group*. London: Routledge.

Lawrence, P. and J. Lorsch. 1967. *Organization and Environment: Managing Differentiation and Integration*. Cambridge MA: Harvard University Press.

Roethlisberger, F. 1977. *The Elusive Phenomena: An Autobiographical Account of My Work in the Field of Organizational Behavior at the Harvard Business School*. Boston MA: Harvard Business School Press.

Roethlisberger, F. and W.J. Dickson. 1939. *Management and the Worker*. Cambridge MA: Harvard University Press.

About the Author

Jay Lorsch has been on the Harvard Business School Faculty since 1964, teaching in the MBA, Doctoral, and Executive Education programs. The Louis E. Kirstein Professor of Human Relations since 1970, Lorsch has held leadership positions at HBS, including: Chair of the Organizational Behavior Area, Senior Associate Dean and Director of Research, Senior Associate Dean and Chair of Executive Education Program, and Chair of the Doctoral Program. Lorsch is the author or coauthor of a number of books including—*Pawns or Potentates: The Reality of America's Corporate Boards*; *Back to the Drawing Board: Designing Corporate Boards for a Complex World*; *Aligning the Stars: How to Succeed When Professionals Drive Results*; and *Organization and Environment*—and over 40 journal articles on the functioning of corporate boards or the leadership of professional service firms. He was elected to the American Academy of Arts and Sciences, and has served on the boards of Benkiser (Netherlands), The Brunswick Corporation, and Computer Associates.

Index

OTHER TITLES IN THE HUMAN RESOURCE MANAGEMENT AND ORGANIZATIONAL BEHAVIOR COLLECTION

Michael J. Provitera, Barry University and Michael Edmondson, Editors

- *11 Secrets of Nonprofit Excellence* by Kathleen Stauffer
- *The Nonprofit Imagineers* by Ben Vorspan
- *At Home With Work* by Nyla Naseer
- *Improv to Improve Your Leadership Team* by Candy Campbell
- *Leadership In Disruptive Times* by Sattar Bawany
- *The Intrapreneurship Formula* by Sandra Lam
- *Navigating Conflict* by Lynne Curry
- *Innovation Soup* by Sanjay Puligadda and Don Waisanen
- *The Aperture for Modern CEOs* by Sylvana Storey
- *The Future of Human Resources* by Tim Baker
- *Change Fatigue Revisited* by Richard Dool and Tahsin I. Alam
- *Championing the Cause of Leadership* by Ted Meyer
- *Embracing Ambiguity* by Michael Edmondson
- *Breaking the Proactive Paradox* by Tim Baker
- *The Modern Trusted Advisor* by Nancy MacKay and Alan Weiss

Concise and Applied Business Books

The Collection listed above is one of 30 business subject collections that Business Expert Press has grown to make BEP a premiere publisher of print and digital books. Our concise and applied books are for...

- Professionals and Practitioners
- Faculty who adopt our books for courses
- Librarians who know that BEP's Digital Libraries are a unique way to offer students ebooks to download, not restricted with any digital rights management
- Executive Training Course Leaders
- Business Seminar Organizers

Business Expert Press books are for anyone who needs to dig deeper on business ideas, goals, and solutions to everyday problems. Whether one print book, one ebook, or buying a digital library of 110 ebooks, we remain the affordable and smart way to be business smart. For more information, please visit www.businessexpertpress.com, or contact sales@businessexpertpress.com.

www.ingramcontent.com/pod-product-compliance
Lightning Source LLC
Chambersburg PA
CBHW061327220326
41599CB00026B/5068